PENGUIN BOOKS

THE 125 BEST RECIPES EVER

Loyd Grossman was born in Boston and raised in Massachusetts. A successful broadcaster, journalist and restaurant critic, he has contributed to most leading British publications, including *The Times* and *Tatler*. Since 1990 he has presented BBC1's *Masterchef*, the most popular food programme in British television history. He lives in London with his wife, two daughters and two dogs.

Loyd Grossman
The 125 best recipes ever

PENGUIN BOOKS

PENGUIN BOOKS

Published by the Penguin Group
Penguin Books Ltd, 27 Wrights Lane, London w8 5tz, England
Penguin Putnam Inc., 375 Hudson Street, New York, New York 10014, USA
Penguin Books Australia Ltd, Ringwood, Victoria, Australia
Penguin Books Canada Ltd, 10 Alcorn Avenue, Toronto, Ontario, Canada m4v 3b2
Penguin Books (NZ) Ltd, Private Bag 102902, NSMC, Auckland, New Zealand

Penguin Books Ltd, Registered Offices: Harmondsworth, Middlesex, England

First published by Michael Joseph 1998
Published in Penguin Books 1999
10 9 8 7 6 5 4 3 2 1

This selection and all introductions copyright © Loyd Grossman, 1998
Photographs copyright © Jean Cazals, 1998
All rights reserved

The acknowledgements on pages 238–40 constitute an extension of this copyright page

The moral right of the author has been asserted

Set in Meta and Monotype Bembo
Printed by Jarrold Book Printing Ltd, Norfolk

Introduction

To say that your mother is a good cook is one of the mantras of filial piety. My mother didn't particularly enjoy cooking but she was very good at it none the less, producing what we might now call 'fusion' cooking – namely a pretty confusing cultural hybrid, which drew on both her New England and Eastern European Jewish backgrounds. Born in 1891, my father was from a generation of men who disdained the work of the kitchen and preferred to think of cooking as a mystery they were disinclined to solve. I never once saw my father so much as make toast. In fact, I have inherited his taste for cold toast, developed because in the days of his Victorian childhood toast was brought to the breakfast room from far-off kitchens. As a child I had no interest in the kitchen at all unless I wanted to get something out of the fridge. The transformation of the kitchen into the 'common room' of the house is a recent phenomenon. Although my father, brother and I were not interested in cooking, we were all extremely enthusiastic about eating, and I was regularly taken to restaurants even when still in my Moses basket.

Julia Child, to my mind, still the greatest of all television cooks, taught me how to cook. Well, not really. But one wet London weekend in the late Seventies I holed up in my flat with a large bag of groceries and a book: *Mastering the Art of French Cooking* by Julia and her sidekicks, Louise Bertholle and Simone Beck. By the end of the weekend I could cook an irreproachable chicken sauté courtesy of Julia and friends. From then on I realized that if you knew how to eat (that is, if you were broadminded about food and familiar with flavours and techniques) and knew how to read, you could learn how to cook. Provided you were reading the right cookbook. I think that Julia Child taught me to cook well: by which I mean that she certainly taught me to cook the sort of food I like to eat.

Another cookbook?

Just what you needed. Over 1,000 cookbooks are published every year and this is one of them. There are already about 20,000 cookbooks in the British Library catalogue. Since Apicius compiled *De re coquinaria libri decem* in the reign of Emperor Augustus, countless recipes have made their way into print.

They are quite obviously the means to an end – something decent to eat – but in an incidental way they can also be works of literature in their own right. Many of the best recipes are well worth reading for pleasure. Elizabeth David, Claudia Roden and Julia Child (to choose just three writers) offer fertile fields for literary criticism. But this book isn't about the art or history of recipe writing; indeed it includes some recipes that are hell to read. I have tried to judge all the recipes in this collection solely on the basis of how useful they are in the modern kitchen. So you will find French *haute cuisine* and traditional British favourites alongside North African, Thai, Chinese, Italian and American dishes. To an extent this glorious jumble reflects the way we eat now. My own taste in recipes is, like anyone else's, conditioned by where I was brought up and where I've travelled, as well as by the skill and 'salesmanship' of the great recipe writers. I very much hope that these recipes will encourage you to try something different and to discover more about the work of lesser-known cookery writers such as Lee Bailey and Irene Kuo.

A Few Culinary Facts of Life

In the last 20 years the geography of cooking has been transformed and the world of flavour redrawn as radically as any political map. The cataclysmic event was the decline and fall of the French culinary empire: an episode as painful to some as the arrival of Attila at the gates of Rome. For over 200 years, through a pantheon of universally revered chefs and a series of canonical cookbooks that were treated like sacred texts, French cultural hegemony was spread throughout the kitchens and dining rooms of the world. Britain gave birth to Nelson and Wellington; the French were as proud of Escoffier and Carême. *Haute cuisine* was established as the model to which all serious cooking had to aspire. From Boston to Berlin, people who took food seriously wanted to produce flawless Tournedos Rossini or Sole Véronique. No more. Who knows what really caused the end of French culinary supremacy. Was it boredom, rebelliousness, worries about health, or our increased exposure to 'ethnic' food thanks to cheaper, easier international travel? The correct answer is probably all of these. Certainly fewer and fewer people now believe that French cooking is any more impressive than Turkish, Japanese or Thai. When Alain Ducasse, the current pope of French cuisine, dared to put an Italian dish, risotto, on his menus, the French culinary establishment gnashed their teeth and wailed, '*Quel horreur!*' Few others took much notice.

It wasn't long after the fall of Communism that a number of Russians became nostalgic for the 'good old days' of the KGB – understandably, because some people find the responsibility that comes with freedom rather irksome. Cooks are no exception. Gone are the 'good old days' when a classically constructed French meal was all that anyone could aspire to. Nowadays cooks and diners have to juggle the competing attractions of a horde of cuisines, flavours and techniques. The results can be disastrous. Putting together a menu in this new age of eclecticism requires intelligence and a certain amount of daring. Look on the bright side: at least you have an unparalleled opportunity to express yourself. But remember, as Alastair Little sagely titled one of his cookbooks: keep it simple.

And God Created the Omelette

At least that's what I said when my five-year-old asked me who made the first omelette. The birth of recipes is often shrouded in mystery. Did the Tatin sisters really make the first upside-down apple tart or were they simply the first cooks to popularize it? The pizza Margherita was 'invented' in Naples in 1889 by Raffaele Esposito in honour of Queen Margherita, but isn't it likely that someone somewhere else had already thought of putting tomato, mozzarella and basil on a pizza? Perhaps it doesn't really matter where recipes come from. Certainly there is no point being too purist about them. At times, the canon of classical recipes seems to be complete, then along comes someone from left field like the Italo-Mexican restaurateur Caesar Cardini who concocts a dish – in his case a salad – that goes on to conquer the culinary world.

The Recipes

All the recipes in this book have been reproduced in their original form (with anglicized terms and measures added to American recipes and metric measures added to older British recipes). I have noted variations on many of them and mentioned useful shortcuts, as well as potential problems that you can avoid. While these recipes are virtuous as they are, I encourage you to tinker with them. They are not immutable or designed to be slavishly copied for ever: I hope that they will inspire you to be creative. This selection is highly personal and so inevitably controversial. It is no more nor less than my hit parade of recipes that I think no cook should be without. Maybe your Auntie Mabel *can* make a better chocolate cake than Ruth Rogers and Rose Gray, but I hope that even when you disagree with some of my choices you will find them stimulating.

Starters, Snacks and Suppers

Oeufs à la Tapenade

Three Mezze

Hummus bi Tahini

Falafel or Ta'Amia

Silver Dollar Corn Cakes

Fried Halloumi Cheese with Lime and Caper Vinaigrette

Pasta e Fagioli

Soupe à l'Oignon

Cream of Spinach Soup

Faki

Curried Butternut Squash Soup

Pissaladière

Huevos Rústicos

Classic Cheese Soufflé

Frittata

Blini

Robert Carrier

Oeufs à la Tapenade

(Great Dishes of the World)

When Bob Carrier and I first met he was living in a pretty flat in Paris just above Allard, a famous, faded and very expensive 'bistro' on the Left Bank. We had a memorable lunch there eating tripe (which I don't like) and drinking Moulin à Vent (which I do). Like me, Bob is American, but he came to Europe with the army during World War II and subsequently drifted into PR before finding cookery. His marketing skills (he came up with the idea of cookery cards) made him one of the very first cooks to achieve mass-market celebrity. He has always had both great taste and a talent for demystifying food. Long before the idea of 'world cuisine', Bob was spreading the word about cosmopolitan cooking. In many ways this recipe typifies his work.

Tapenade pops up on smart menus everywhere in the nineties but is a traditional Provençal dish. Here Bob gives a canonical version of it and then, with an acute eye for fashion, presents it very much as a seventies dish (when this recipe was published) by using it to make stuffed eggs. Today we'd be more likely to place a little quenelle of it alongside some grilled fish. I can eat it by the bucketful.

50g/2oz stoned ripe olives
25g/1oz anchovy fillets
25g/1oz tuna fish
1 teaspoon mustard
25g/1oz capers

4–6 tablespoons olive oil
1 tablespoon cognac
freshly ground black pepper
4 hard-boiled eggs
lettuce, to garnish

Pound stoned ripe olives, anchovy fillets and tuna fish to a smooth paste in a mortar with mustard and capers (called *tapeno* in Provençal, from which this dish gets its name). When the mixture has been blended to a smooth paste, put it through a fine sieve and whisk olive oil into it. Add cognac and black pepper to taste.

To make oeufs à la tapenade: cut hard-boiled eggs in half lengthwise and remove yolks. Blend yolks with tapenade mixture, adding a little more olive oil if necessary; fill egg cavities and serve on a bed of lettuce. The tapenade mixture keeps well in a covered jar and is excellent as a canapé spread.

Anissa Helou

Three Mezze

(Lebanese Cuisine)

I couldn't cite just one recipe from *Lebanese Cuisine*, Anissa Helou's magisterial work on Lebanese food, so I have chosen a small constellation of little dishes that are meant to be eaten together: *mezze*. Many people (including me) find the promiscuous nibbling that kicks off a Lebanese meal one of the culinary turn-ons of all time. Indeed, plenty of *mezze*, lots of different breads from a Middle Eastern delicatessen and a large bowl of salad (cos lettuce, finely chopped radishes, green peppers and tomatoes, dressed in olive oil and lemon juice) makes a stellar supper.

You can grill the aubergines for the *baba ghannooge* but they will taste even better if you are able to barbecue them. Heed Anissa's advice not to overprocess the aubergines (advice worth remembering whenever you switch on the food processor) or you will get a featureless paste: *baba ghannooge* needs a bit of texture. The pomegranate seed garnish sounds a bit fiddly and *de trop*, but do it and add a bit of sparkle to what, despite its outstanding flavour, isn't the world's prettiest dish.

I am not (never have been really) convinced about chicken wings. But Anissa's recipe for Chicken Marinated in Garlic has shown me that they can be very moreish indeed. You may have had buffalo chicken wings in American-style theme bars or restaurants; this is an infinitely better way to cook them. Anissa suggests grilling; I prefer baking them. The megatonnage of garlic (8 cloves for 4 people) makes this a dish for consenting adults only, and a godsend for mouthwash manufacturers.

The Yoghurt and Cucumber Salad couldn't be easier or more refreshing but it's important to salt large cucumbers. This process – known as degorging – draws out excess moisture and gives you a less waterlogged cucumber. You might remember it next time the vicar comes round for tea and you make cucumber sandwiches.

Baba Ghannooge
Aubergine Purée

Serves 4

3 large aubergines (about 300g/11oz each)
3 tablespoons tahini
juice of 1 lemon, or to taste
2 garlic cloves, peeled and crushed
salt to taste

For the garnish:
fresh mint or parsley leaves
paprika or pomegranate seeds (the sour type)
extra virgin olive oil

Prick the aubergines in several places with a small knife or a fork – to stop them from bursting during cooking – and cook whole with stalks on under a hot grill for 25–30 minutes, turning them to expose all sides equally to the heat. When cooked the aubergines should have shrivelled to about half their original size, be very soft to the touch, with blistered skin. If this is not possible, you can bake them in a preheated oven 180°C/350°F/Gas Mark 4 for 45 minutes (or microwave them for 5–6 minutes). However if you use the oven or the microwave methods you will sadly lose the charred taste of the open-fire cooking that is so typically Lebanese.

Cooling your fingers under cold running water, peel and discard the skin of the aubergines while they are still hot and put the flesh in a colander to drain for about 15 minutes.

Cut off and discard the stalks before putting the aubergines in a wide mixing bowl and mashing them with a masher or fork along the grain of the pulp. If you prefer to use a blender, be very careful not to liquidize the aubergines too much. Use the pulse lever; two or three turns will be enough to get the right consistency. If you have no pulse lever, simulate the action by turning your machine on and immediately off again. The purée made with the food processor will be creamier than the handmade one, but just as good.

When the aubergines are mashed, stir in the tahini and salt to taste and mix well. As you are blending the tahini you will notice that the colour of the aubergines becomes lighter. Mix in the lemon juice and crushed garlic. Taste the purée and adjust seasoning if necessary. Garnish with mint or parsley leaves, sprinkle over paprika or pomegranate seeds and drizzle with extra virgin olive oil.

Chicken Wings Marinated in Garlic

Serves 4

8 big chicken wings or 12 small ones

For the marinade:

8 large garlic cloves, peeled and crushed

2 tablespoons extra virgin olive oil

juice of 1 lemon, or to taste

1/8 teaspoon ground cinnamon

1/2 teaspoon ground allspice

1/4 teaspoon finely ground black pepper

pinch of cayenne pepper (optional)

salt to taste

Rinse the chicken wings in cold water and pat them dry with kitchen paper. Put the crushed garlic in a large mixing bowl and stir in the olive oil, lemon juice and seasonings. Add the chicken wings, coat them well with the marinade and leave for an hour, turning them over occasionally.

Grill or barbecue the wings for about 10 minutes on each side or until they are nearly charcoaled and crispy. Alternatively you can bake them for about 30 minutes in a hot oven, turning them over halfway through so that they are crisp on both sides. Serve hot with a garlic dip.

Yoghurt and Cucumber Salad

Serves 4

300g/11oz small cucumbers, quartered and
thinly sliced

450g/1lb yoghurt

1 tablespoon dried mint

1 garlic clove, peeled and crushed

salt to taste

If you cannot find small cucumbers and are using large ones, sprinkle the slices with salt, leave to sweat for 30 minutes, then rinse under cold water and pat dry with kitchen paper.

Put the yoghurt in a salad bowl, stir in the dried mint and salt to taste and leave for 15 minutes or until the dried mint has softened. Fold in the sliced cucumber and crushed garlic. Taste, adjust seasoning if necessary, and serve at room temperature.

Hummus bi Tahini

(Mediterranean Cookery)

Claudia Roden, a daughter of the once-flourishing community of Jews from Alexandria on the Mediterranean coast of Egypt, has written brilliantly and beautifully about the food of the region ever since her majestic *A Book of Middle Eastern Food* first appeared in 1968. Alas, Middle Eastern food is still rather marginal to most people's cooking and eating, with the exception of hummus – the chickpea dip that you can buy at nearly every corner shop and supermarket. It is an almost universally popular way of getting your daily garlic injection and if you think it is little more than a mass-produced commodity, treat yourself and prepare some at home. You can then make it as fierce as you like and sit by yourself until the effects wear off.

You could use tinned chickpeas to make hummus but I would urge you to try dried ones instead. Claudia advises cooking them for about an hour: I would bring them to a rolling boil first and cook them for about 10 minutes before reducing the heat to a simmer for Claudia's hour. They may even take longer than this, but are blessedly difficult to overcook.

Hummus is usually dressed with a dusting of cayenne pepper. If you are feeling adventurous, go to an Iranian food shop to buy some of the delicious, astringent dried herb, sumac, and add a pinch of that, too.

Serves 4–6

100g/4oz chickpeas, soaked for a few hours
juice of 2 lemons
3 tablespoons tahini
2 garlic cloves, crushed
salt

For the garnish:
1 tablespoon olive oil
1 teaspoon paprika
a few sprigs of parsley, finely chopped

Drain the chickpeas and simmer in fresh water for about an hour or until tender. Reserve the cooking water.

Process the chickpeas in a blender with the lemon juice, tahini, garlic and salt and enough of the cooking liquid to obtain a soft creamy consistency.

Serve on a flat plate, garnished with a dribble of olive oil, a dusting of paprika (this is usually done in the shape of a cross) and a little parsley.

Claudia Roden

Falafel or Ta'Amia

(Mediterranean Cookery)

In the days when my student friends and I wandered around Cambridge, Massachusetts, busking, we ate a lot of falafel. Unlike many of the things I liked in the late Sixties – tie-dyes, Canned Heat, Jean-Luc Godard films – my taste for falafel remains.

It is popular throughout the Middle East but originates from Egypt, so who better to give the definitive recipe than Claudia Roden, who was born and raised in Cairo? She uses dried broad beans, but if these are difficult to find you could substitute chickpeas.

It is insulting to compare falafel to that rather hopeless product, the vegeburger, but I suppose that is what they are: crisply fried, highly seasoned Middle Eastern fast food that you can eat as part of a first course or – most deliciously, as Claudia suggests – shoved into a pitta bread with some crisp lettuce and a drizzle of thinned tahini. I would also add either a few thinly sliced gherkins or, better yet, some pickled green chillies. Claudia suggests eating falafel for breakfast. I've done so in Cairo and they make an excellent kickstart to the day if you've stayed up too late the night before watching the bellydancing.

Serves 10

500g/1lb 2oz skinned broad beans, soaked overnight
salt and pepper
2 teaspoons cumin
pinch of cayenne (optional)
1 teaspoon bicarbonate of soda

6–10 garlic cloves
large bunch of coriander, finely chopped
large bunch of parsley, finely chopped
1 large onion, very finely chopped
4–5 spring onions, very finely chopped
sunflower or other light vegetable oil

Drain the beans well and put through a food processor until they form a very soft paste. The secret of success is to have a paste so smooth and soft that it holds together in the frying oil. Add salt and pepper, cumin, cayenne and bicarbonate of soda and let the mixture rest for an hour.

Add the rest of the ingredients, using plenty of herbs, about 50g/2oz or more. If you chop the onion in the food processor make sure that you drain off any juices. Knead the mixture well with your hands.

Take small lumps of paste, roll them into balls and flatten them into cakes about 5cm (2 inches) in diameter and 5mm (¼ inch) thick. Fry the cakes in hot oil, turning them over once, until they are crisp and brown. Lift them out with a slotted spoon and drain on kitchen paper. Reheat in the oven before serving.

Serve, if you like, in pitta bread with chopped lettuce and tomatoes, and tahini diluted with water and lemon juice and seasoned with salt and pepper as a sauce.

Julee Rosso

Silver Dollar Corn Cakes

(Fresh Start)

I am a great lover of all manner of pancakes, whether it's a stack of thick American pancakes with banana ice cream or unsalted butter, crispy potato pancakes with apple sauce, or thick and bitter buckwheat *blini* with soured cream and smoked salmon. I'm only let down by crêpes, which I find remarkably insipid unless eaten painted with jam straight from the griddle of a street vendor in France. Julee Rosso has come up with some all-American corn cakes, which you can serve as a sweet breakfast dish or a savoury side dish. You could use frozen corn (never tinned) for this recipe but fresh corn is better. Stand an ear of corn upright with the stalk end on your chopping board. Take a sharp knife and cut straight down the cob. Kernels will fly everywhere – if you're lucky most of them will land on the board.

You can find cornmeal in Indian and Caribbean food shops and large supermarkets, otherwise use fine polenta. Canola is what Americans call rapeseed oil, but any bland cooking oil (such as sun-flower) will do. Buttermilk is another common American – and Irish – ingredient which requires a trip to a large supermarket. Aside from working well in this recipe it improves all manner of bread and cakes, giving them a light, moist texture.

Maple syrup is an expensive product, since it takes 35 gallons of maple tree sap to make one gallon of syrup. Its flavour is incomparable, with a complex sweetness featuring bitter caramel notes. Do not buy 'maple-flavour' syrup, which is a banal, synthetic concoction. Most big supermarkets stock Canadian or Vermont (I prefer Vermont) maple syrup. It is also fabulous poured over ice cream or into porridge.

To make a savoury version of these pancakes just omit the maple syrup and simmer the corn in a little water, then drain. Savoury corn pancakes are delicious with grilled chicken, lamb or beef and particularly nice with a little soured cream and a spoonful of hot red or green Mexican salsa. You can make a batch up in advance and freeze them.

Serves 8

1¹/₂ cups [*350ml/12fl oz*] maple syrup
2 cups [*225g/8oz*] fresh or frozen corn kernels
¹/₂ cup [*50g/2oz*] cornmeal
2 tablespoons flour
¹/₂ teaspoon baking soda [*bicarbonate of soda*]

¹/₄ teaspoon salt
1¹/₂ teaspoons canola oil
³/₄ cup [*175ml/6fl oz*] buttermilk
1 large egg, lightly beaten

In a small saucepan, heat the maple syrup and 1 cup of the corn kernels over low heat for 10 to 15 minutes, until the corn is tender and the mixture is heated through.

In a bowl, combine the cornmeal, flour, baking soda and salt. Stir in the oil, buttermilk and egg until just combined. Gently fold in the remaining corn kernels.

Lightly spray a nonstick skillet [*frying pan*] with vegetable oil spray and heat over medium heat until a few drops of water scattered on the pan evaporate quickly. Drop 1 tablespoon of the batter for each cake into the skillet and cook for 1 minute per side, or until lightly golden. Spoon the warm maple syrup and corn over the cakes and serve.

Delia Smith

Fried Halloumi Cheese with Lime and Caper Vinaigrette

(Delia Smith's Summer Collection)

No British cook has been more trusted and followed since Mrs Beeton. Although Delia Smith is firmly rooted in the basics of British food, she has increasingly introduced Mediterranean tastes and methods into her repertoire, as this recipe demonstrates. Her gentle but insistent step-by-step expository style has banished the fear of cooking from many households.

Halloumi is a very useful cheese and, as Delia points out, 'has a reasonably long shelf-life, which means that you can always have a pack tucked away in the refrigerator'. The last time I bought a pack of this tangy, slightly rubbery Greek cheese I noticed that its sell-by date was a year ahead. You can slice halloumi and shove it under a hot grill, then serve it with some strong green olive oil trickled on top. Or you can dust it lightly with flour and fry it, as Delia does. The dressing is as unGreek as they come but works well with the fried cheese. You can serve this just as recommended, with pitta bread or Greek bread, but I like to put the fried cheese on a little heap of green salad. As with other Greek or Greekish recipes this may be the time to treat yourself to a glass of cold retsina, the resinated wine that the wine writer Harry Waugh once described as a drink that many people felt was 'an acquired taste not worth acquiring'.

Serves 2 as a light lunch or 4 as a starter

1 halloumi cheese

2 tablespoons olive oil

2 tablespoons well-seasoned flour

For the dressing:

juice and zest of 1 lime

1 tablespoon white wine vinegar

1 heaped tablespoon capers, drained

1 clove garlic, finely chopped

1 heaped teaspoon grain mustard

1 heaped tablespoon chopped fresh coriander leaves

2 tablespoons extra virgin olive oil

salt and freshly milled black pepper

To garnish:

a few sprigs of coriander

First of all unwrap the cheese and pat it dry with kitchen paper. Then, using a sharp knife, slice it into eight slices, including the ends. Now prepare the dressing by simply whisking all the ingredients together in a small mixing-bowl.

When you're ready to serve the halloumi, heat the oil in a frying pan over a medium heat. When the oil is really hot, press each slice of cheese into seasoned flour to coat it on both sides, then add them to the hot pan as they are done – they take 1 minute on each side to cook, so by the time the last one's in it will almost be time to turn the first one over. They need to be a good golden colour on each side.

Serve them straight away on warmed plates with the dressing poured over. This is good served with lightly toasted pitta bread or Greek bread with toasted sesame seeds.

Ann and Franco Taruschio

Pasta e Fagioli
Pasta and Bean Soup

(Leaves from The Walnut Tree)

An old roadside pub in Abergavenny is an unusual place to spread the good news about classic Italian cooking but that is where Franco and Ann Taruschio made their home and created their restaurant The Walnut Tree. Elizabeth David was a great fan of Franco's cooking and the restaurant attracts any number of long-distance food pilgrims, alongside a steady core of local regulars who must be as pleased as they are bemused that this small corner of Italy should exist in South Wales. I have always eaten extremely well at The Walnut Tree and I am a great admirer of Ann and Franco's writing, too: no nonsense, no chat, just get on with it and produce something wonderful to eat.

Pasta e fagioli was born in Venice but has been widely embraced throughout Italy. No soup is more reliable an example of good, simple everyday food that still manages to be awesome when made with care.

Two worthy tricks to note in this recipe: first, wrapping the rosemary in muslin to protect eaters from mouthfuls of chewy needles; secondly, the Italian custom of puréeing half the cooked beans and returning them to the soup for a smooth, thick texture. Don't forget the trickle of olive oil and pinch of chilli flakes at the end. Many cooks also like to add a little freshly grated Parmesan as well.

Serves 4

300g/11oz fresh borlotti beans or 200g/7oz
   dried borlotti beans, presoaked

1 ham hock

1 onion

2 cloves garlic

2 stalks celery

1 sprig rosemary

2 sprigs parsley

120ml/4fl oz extra virgin olive oil

200g/7oz small tubular pasta

freshly ground black pepper, and salt if
   necessary

dried chilli flakes

Put 2 litres/3$^{1}/_{2}$ pints of water in a heavy saucepan which has a well fitting lid, add the borlotti beans, ham hock, onion, garlic, celery, rosemary (wrapped in muslin), parsley and olive oil. Bring to the boil, lower the heat and gently cook the beans for 1$^{1}/_{2}$ hours. Discard the ham hock and rosemary, remove the vegetables and blend them. Put half of the beans through a food mill or liquidizer and return the purée to the soup of beans and vegetables. Do not replace the lid. Season with freshly ground black pepper and check the seasoning: salt may not be necessary. Bring back to the boil. Add the pasta and cook until *al dente*. Serve with a dash of extra virgin olive oil and a pinch of chilli pepper to taste.

Patience Gray and Primrose Boyd

Soupe à l'Oignon

(Plats du Jour)

Scholarly cooks will be familiar with Patience Gray's outstanding book *Honey from a Weed* but her earlier joint effort *Plats du Jour*, with its charming period alternative title *or Foreign Food*, is full of well written and researched recipes and shows that the rediscovery of French and Italian cookery by fifties Britain involved more than just the gospel according to Elizabeth David.

Onion soup has become frightfully unfashionable. A pity really, as it is so good and was once the most obvious sign that 'foreign' cooking was on the menu. I guess that today's benchmark soups are so highly wrought and fantastic that onion soup seems distinctly rough trade, which after all is part of its charm. It is a soup designed to be eaten by hungover *garagistes* smoking Gîtanes: definitely more Gérard Depardieu than Catherine Deneuve. As Patience Gray and Primrose Boyd vividly describe it, 'It is a well-known pick-me-up in France for those who have drunk too well, and is an example of the miraculous powers of the onion.'

When Les Halles was still the working marketplace of central Paris you could order a bowl of onion soup in the middle of the night at one of the many restaurants that stayed open round the clock to cater for market workers. A 2 a.m. bowl of onion soup was ritualistically drunk by many romantic tourists like me on my first visit to Paris and must have seemed rather hilarious to the locals. Vegetarians can make this recipe substituting a good, strong, homemade vegetable stock and the resulting soup will be delicious but lacking that dark, slightly thuggish quality that makes *soupe à l'oignon* such a great dish.

about 2oz [*50g*] fresh butter or beef dripping
1lb [*450g*] finely sliced Spanish onions
1 small bay leaf
1 clove

salt, black pepper and brown sugar
2 pints [*1.2 litres*] of beef stock
some dried slices of bread
grated cheese

Melt most of the butter (or dripping) in the bottom of the *marmite* [*earthenware casserole*] and fry the onion slices until they are transparent and golden. At the same time, put in the bay leaf, and crumble the knob of the clove over the frying mixture. Add salt, a pinch of brown sugar and some ground black pepper. Then heat the beef stock and pour it on to the onion and butter mixture in the casserole. Simmer the soup for at least half an hour, and about 10 minutes before it is to be served fry the dry slices of bread in the rest of the butter in a separate pan. When they are golden, sprinkle grated cheese over each side of them and place one in the bottom of each hot soup bowl. Pour in the soup, and serve more grated cheese separately. This should properly be Gruyère.

Alternatively, the soup can be poured into bowls, the fried bread sprinkled with cheese being floated on the top and the bowls placed under the grill for a few minutes to brown the cheese.

George Lang

Cream of Spinach Soup

(The Cuisine of Hungary)

There is no more interesting example of the cultural significance of food than the way in which Communist regimes have suppressed the cooking of their 'bourgeois' predecessors. Over 40 years of totalitarian rule in Hungary nearly destroyed a complex and fascinating cuisine. It was preserved largely in expatriate kitchens around the world and through the work of a few scholarly writers such as George Lang. In his book *The Cuisine of Hungary* he begins his chapter on soups by noting that, 'According to the rules of the French kitchen, you're not supposed to start *déjeuner* with a soup course. In Hungary it is different; there soup is an essential part of the midday meal.' I suppose that also helps to explain the once-heard English adage that 'no gentleman eats soup at luncheon'.

Out of Lang's many soup recipes I like this one best. It so clearly illustrates his rules of Hungarian soup making: 'no stocks generally, no fancy spices, no cognac or sherry or other taste crutches'. If you don't have any chicken fat to hand, and you probably don't, brown the onions in a mixture of butter and oil. The garnish of hard-boiled eggs and crispy bacon is novel and delicious. Vegetarians could skip the bacon.

Serves 8

900g/2lb spinach, well washed
1 teaspoon salt
2 large onions, minced or grated
4 tablespoons chicken fat

6 tablespoons flour
500ml/17fl oz single cream
4 hard-boiled eggs, sliced
bacon crumbles (optional)

Cook the spinach in 1.75 litres/3 pints of water with the salt for 5 minutes. Strain; save the water. Rub spinach to a pulp through a sieve or purée in a blender.

Brown onions in fat, add the flour and blend. Cook for a few more minutes.

Stir in 250ml/8fl oz of the cool spinach liquid and cook, stirring, until thick and smooth. Add the remaining liquid and the puréed spinach. Heat to boiling.

Remove from heat and blend in the cream. Garnish with the egg slices and crumbled crisp bacon.

Aglaia Kremezi

Faki
Lentil Soup

(The Foods of Greece)

My mother cooked excellent lentil soup in the winter, which she served Eastern European style with some sliced frankfurters in it. But the best lentil soup I ever tasted was dished up in late September in a small taverna on the Greek island of Ithaca, which the classically inclined will know as the home of Odysseus. Aglaia Kremezi tells us that lentil soup, or *faki*, was 'the Ancient Greeks' favourite winter soup. They considered lentils to be especially nourishing, so the painter Agatharcus depicted Orestes eating lentils when he was recovering from illness.' Even today lentils are reputed to give farmers strength for the harvest, and in many cultures are thought to be harbingers of financial good fortune. This recipe is perhaps a much fuller-flavoured lentil soup than you've tasted before, powerfully spiked with bay leaves, mustard and a hefty amount of vinegar. When Aglaia Kremezi calls for tomato purée I suggest you substitute passata, while her tomato paste is what British cooks know as tomato purée. You can serve this as a first course but it makes an even better supper on a cold night, with plenty of crusty bread and, for even more atmosphere, a bottle of retsina.

Serves 6–8

2 cups [*400g/14oz*] **large green lentils**
1¹/₂ quarts [*1.5 litres/2¹/₂ pints*] **water**
3 **bay leaves**
¹/₂ cup [*120ml/4fl oz*] **olive oil**
3–4 **medium onions, chopped**
3–4 **cloves garlic, finely chopped**
¹/₂–1 **fresh chilli pepper, minced**

3 cups [*750ml/1¹/₄ pints*] **fresh or good-quality canned tomato purée**
2 tablespoons **tomato paste**
1 tablespoon **dry mustard**
sea salt
¹/₃ cup [*85ml/3fl oz*] **red wine vinegar, or more**
¹/₂ cup [*20g/³/₄ oz*] **chopped fresh dill**

Rinse the lentils and place in a large pot with the water and the bay leaves. Bring to a boil, strain, and discard the water. Add more water and bring to a boil again, then reduce the heat and simmer for 20 to 30 minutes.

In a skillet [*frying pan*], heat the olive oil over medium heat and sauté the onions until soft, about 3 minutes. Add the garlic and chilli pepper and transfer the sautéed vegetables and cooking oil to the pot with the lentils. Add the tomato purée and paste and the mustard, stir well, and continue simmering for another 30 minutes, or until lentils are tender, adding a little more water if necessary.

Season with salt and vinegar, and remove the bay leaves. Taste and add more salt and vinegar if needed.

Serve hot, sprinkling each soup plate with fresh dill.

Julee Rosso and Sheila Lukins

Curried Butternut Squash Soup

(The Silver Palate Cookbook)

A lot of squashes and pumpkins (many of them from Australia or South Africa) have started appearing in British supermarkets and greengrocers'. Squash keeps a long time. You needn't store it in the fridge and a few squashes will liven up the look of your kitchen. However, unlike gourds they are not merely weird and decorative and they are much easier to prepare than their less manageable cousin, the pumpkin. For my money, butternut squash is the best of the lot. At home as a child, I used to eat a lot of butternut squash in autumn and winter, boiled, then mashed with a generous amount of butter and seasoned with plenty of black pepper and a little nutmeg. It is excellent served alongside roast chicken or turkey, with a chicken or beef stew, or with one of the heftier fish such as halibut.

Squash has recently been wearing trendier clothes and you may have seen it in restaurant dishes such as butternut squash risotto. When served as a vegetable nowadays it is more likely to be roasted: simply peel it, cut into chunks (remove the seeds, which all cluster in the fat end of squash), splash with olive oil and season with salt and pepper, then roast in a fairly hot oven until tender. Some people add a few cloves of garlic or sprinkle the squash with a little brown sugar.

This slightly more time-consuming recipe makes a delicious winter soup, not unlike parsnip but with more depth of flavour. While apples in savoury dishes usually give me the horrors they actually do work in this recipe, which comes from *The Silver Palate Cookbook*, an indispensable addition to the kitchen for every enlightened American family in the eighties. It is one of those cookbooks that seem to have progressed effortlessly from cult to classic status. I use my copy frequently and have never been let down by Rosso and Lukins' practical advice and sound instinct for interesting flavours.

Serves 4–6

4 tablespoons [*50g/2oz*] sweet [unsalted] butter

2 cups [*225g/8oz*] finely chopped yellow onions

4 to 5 teaspoons curry powder

2 medium-size butternut squash (about 3 pounds [*1.5kg*] altogether)

3 cups [*750ml/1 ¼ pints*] chicken stock

2 apples, peeled, cored and chopped

1 cup [*250ml/8fl oz*] apple juice

salt and freshly ground black pepper, to taste

1 shredded unpeeled Granny Smith apple (garnish)

Melt the butter in a pot. Add chopped onions and curry powder and cook, covered, over low heat until onions are tender, about 25 minutes.

Meanwhile peel the squash (a regular vegetable peeler works best), scrape out the seeds and chop the flesh.

When onions are tender, pour in the stock, add squash and apples and bring to a boil.

Reduce heat and simmer, partially covered, until squash and apples are very tender, about 25 minutes.

Pour the soup through a strainer [*sieve*], reserving liquid, and transfer the solids to the bowl of a food processor fitted with a steel blade, or use a food mill fitted with a medium disc. Add 1 cup [*250ml/8fl oz*] of the cooking stock and process until smooth.

Return puréed soup to the pot and add apple juice and additional cooking liquid, about 2 cups [*500ml/17fl oz*], until the soup is of the desired consistency.

Season to taste with salt and pepper, simmer briefly to heat through, and serve immediately, garnished with shredded apple.

Claudia Roden

Pissaladière

(Mediterranean Cookery)

A *pissaladière* is emphatically not just an onion, anchovy and olive pizza. It's an altogether different creature, with a distinctive sweet yet savoury flavour that comes from the interaction between the caramelized onions and the salty anchovies. I would go for the bigger quantity of onions suggested in the recipe, and use a little more oil.

This dish isn't very technically demanding provided you're not fussed about making dough. Don't get lulled into a false sense of security, though. Stewing onions so that they caramelize properly may not be rocket science but it does require plenty of patience and care. Don't rush, and don't settle for undercooked onions either. Fresh yeast works best for the base but you could substitute either dried or easy-blend yeast. In fact, if you are nervous about making dough you could use frozen puff pastry for the base and, although it won't be a *pissaladière*, it will still taste pretty darned good.

Serves 6

For the dough:	For the filling:
250g/9oz plain flour	**1–2kg/2¼–4½lb onions, thinly sliced**
1 egg, beaten	**3–4 tablespoons olive oil**
¾ teaspoon salt	**salt and pepper**
15g/½oz fresh yeast, or 1½ teaspoons dried yeast	**2 teaspoons mixed fresh herbs such as basil, thyme and rosemary, chopped**
¼ teaspoon sugar	**12 or more anchovy fillets**
85ml/3fl oz warm water	**a few black olives, stoned and halved**
a few drops of olive oil	

To make the bread dough, sift the flour into a bowl and make a well in the centre. Put the beaten egg and salt in the well. Put the yeast, sugar and water in a bowl and leave it until it froths. Then gradually stir the yeast mixture into the flour, mixing it in with your fingers to form a ball of soft dough. Add a little flour if it is too sticky and knead well with your hands for 10 minutes or until the dough is smooth and elastic. Pour a drop or two of olive oil on the dough and turn it in your hands so that it becomes lightly oiled all over. Cover with a damp cloth and leave to rise in a warm place for an hour or until it doubles in bulk.

While the dough is rising make the filling. Cook the onions in the olive oil in a covered pan on a very low flame, stirring occasionally, for 40 minutes or until they are very soft. Add the salt, pepper and herbs and continue to cook for a few minutes longer. Cut the anchovy fillets in half lengthways.

Preheat the oven to 190°C/375°F/Gas Mark 5. Grease a pie plate or flan dish about 35cm (14 inches) in diameter with oil. Punch the dough down, knead it lightly and press it into the pie plate with the palms of your hands. Spread the onion mixture over the dough and make a lattice pattern of anchovy fillets on top. Put half an olive in the middle of each square. Let the dough rise again for 10–15 minutes, then bake for 25–30 minutes or until the bread base is cooked. Serve hot.

Rick Bayless

Huevos Rústicos

(Rick Bayless's Mexican Kitchen)

This is a slight variation on *huevos rancheros*, a classic Mexican dish which I first ate at the Pink Turtle Café in the Beverly Wiltshire Hotel, an old-time film moguls' hangout in Beverly Hills. The combination of fried egg and punchy tomato salsa makes a splendidly relaxed dish for brunch or supper. As Rick Bayless writes, 'On Sunday morning or evening, food should be what you want to eat, not what you feel you ought to.' Bayless is one of the English-speaking world's great codifiers and interpreters of Mexican cooking, walking his readers through the recipes in a detailed, handholding, but uncondescending way. In Europe we are almost completely unexposed to Mexican food, which tends to crop up only in parody form as an accompaniment to too many margaritas. It is a rich, weird and stimulating cuisine, with many flavours and techniques worth exploring.

Mexican ingredients are still rather difficult to find in British shops, although more upmarket delicatessens are now selling a reasonable range of dried chillies. Fresh jalapeños are difficult to get hold of so you'll have to use the not very flavourful tinned ones or substitute a different variety of fresh chilli. You probably won't be able to get Mexican cheese but feta (the blander French or German version) is an excellent substitute. Frozen corn tortillas are surprisingly easy to find. They keep well in the freezer. Thaw and then quickly heat them in a very hot dry frying pan as Bayless suggests – no more than 45 seconds as you just want to heat them through, not grill them. If you're making these *huevos rústicos* for supper, serve them with nothing more than a simple green salad and a bottle or two of very cold Mexican lager.

Serves 4 as a nice breakfast (if you're also serving fruit, breads or beans), perhaps 2 if you want something really substantial

4 corn tortillas

1 tablespoon vegetable or olive oil

4 eggs

2 tablespoons finely crumbled Mexican *queso añejo*, dry feta or Parmesan

For the Essential Roasted Tomato-Jalapeño Salsa:

1 pound [450g] (2 medium-large or 6–8 plum) ripe tomatoes

2 to 3 fresh jalapeño chillies

3 garlic cloves, unpeeled

salt, a scant 1/2 teaspoon

1/2 small white onion, finely chopped, plus a little extra for garnish

a scant 1/2 cup [15g/1/2oz] chopped cilantro [*coriander*], plus a few sprigs for garnish

Making Essential Roasted Tomato-Jalapeño Salsa: roast the tomatoes on a baking sheet 4 inches [*10cm*] below a very hot broiler [*grill*] until blackened on one side, about 6 minutes, then flip and roast the other side. Cool and peel, collecting all the juices with the tomatoes. While the tomatoes are roasting, roast the chillies and unpeeled garlic directly on an ungreased griddle or heavy skillet [*frying pan*] over medium heat, turning occasionally, until soft (they'll blacken in spots: 5 to 10 minutes for the chillies, about 15 minutes for the garlic). Cool, then pull the stems from the chillies and peel the garlic.

In a large mortar (or small food processor/grinder), pound (or whir) the chillies, garlic and salt into a coarse-textured purée. Add the juicy tomatoes (a few at a time, if using a mortar) and work them into a coarse, rich-textured salsa. Rinse the onion in a strainer [*sieve*] under cold water, shake off the excess and add to the tomato mixture, along with the cilantro. Taste and season with salt.

The tortillas: lightly toast the tortillas directly over a gas flame or in an ungreased nonstick skillet over an electric burner, turning once, until heated through, 30 to 45 seconds. Wrap up in a thick clean towel to keep warm.

Finishing the dish: in a medium-size saucepan bring the salsa to a simmer, cover and keep warm over low heat.

Heat the oil in a large well-seasoned or nonstick skillet (you'll need a lid) over medium to medium-low heat. Crack the eggs into the skillet, cover and cook 1 minute. Uncover and continue cooking until the whites are set but the yolks are still runny, 1 to 2 minutes more (at least that's how I like them).

Lay a tortilla on each of 4 warm plates. Top each tortilla with an egg and spoon the warm salsa over everything, keeping the yolks uncovered if you like that look. Sprinkle with a little onion and the cheese, decorate with cilantro sprigs and the *huevos rústicos* are ready.

Josceline Dimbleby

Classic Cheese Soufflé

(The Cook's Companion)

Josceline Dimbleby is an excellent singer, originally destined for the stage, who – thankfully for cooks – ended up in the kitchen. As a cookery writer she is one of the very best at clearly and patiently explaining tricky operations. There are more than enough lame anecdotes about collapsing soufflés ruining important dinner parties, and many cooks are needlessly terrified by the idea of making what is, after all, little more than a sauce with some beaten egg whites mixed in. Anyone can make a soufflé, although it helps to have an oven with a glass door. I wouldn't say that being able to turn out a decent soufflé is an absolute requirement for any serious cook – indeed soufflés are rather out of favour these days – but they are great fun and make excellent curtain raisers. As Jossy writes, 'the dramatic rise of a soufflé and its brief moment of exquisite glory are unparalleled.' If you master her basic recipe you will boldly go on to her unconventional variations, such as puréed parsnips with Indian spices or chive and wholegrain mustard.

Serves 2 as a main course or 3–4 as a starter

25g/1oz butter

3 tablespoons plain flour

½ teaspoon curry powder, English mustard or ground nutmeg

pinch of cayenne pepper

200ml/7fl oz milk

50g/2oz mature Cheddar cheese, grated

25g/1oz Parmesan cheese, grated

4 eggs, separated

1–2 extra egg whites (optional)

salt and black pepper

To make the base sauce, melt the butter in a medium-sized saucepan, then stir in the flour and the curry powder, English mustard or ground nutmeg and cayenne pepper. Cook for 1 minute, stirring constantly until the roux has a sandy texture.

Gradually add the milk, stirring until the sauce thickens, then simmer for 2 minutes. Remove from the heat, mix in all but a spoonful of the 2 cheeses until melted, then beat in the egg yolks. Season well with salt and black pepper.

Whisk the egg whites until they form stiff, but not dry, peaks. (Include the extra egg whites if you want a very high soufflé.) Beat 1 tablespoon of egg white into the sauce to loosen it. This makes it easier to fold in the whites without losing any air.

With a large metal spoon, gently fold in the rest of the beaten egg whites, turning the spoon in a figure-of-eight movement. Butter a 1.2 litre/2 pint soufflé dish and coat the sides with dry breadcrumbs to help the soufflé 'climb' up the side of the dish as it rises during cooking.

Spoon the soufflé into the prepared dish and sprinkle the top with the reserved cheese. Bake in a preheated oven, 190°C/375°F/Gas Mark 5 for 20–25 minutes, until well risen and golden brown – the soufflé should wobble very slightly when shaken. Serve instantly.

Whisking egg whites
Soufflés rise to their impressive heights because of the air trapped in whisked egg whites. Using a food processor to whisk egg white will not produce enough volume for a soufflé, though electric whisks or rotary beaters give excellent results. The best-textured egg whites, however, are produced by whisking with a balloon whisk in a large copper bowl. Lift the whisk out of the whites each time, using large circular sweeps of your arm to incorporate as much air as possible. A small amount of salt helps to make the white more stable and so able to trap the air longer.

Hints and tips
Any trace of grease in the whisking bowl will prevent the egg whites from rising properly, so wash it out before use with very hot water and a drop of detergent or wipe with a little vinegar. Dry the bowl thoroughly. Whisked egg whites should form slightly soft peaks. If the whites are beaten too much, they will be dry and will not fold well into the sauce.

The classic cheese soufflé recipe (above) can be cooked in individual ramekin dishes instead of one large dish: place the ramekins on a baking sheet and cook for about 12 minutes only. Individual unbaked soufflés can be frozen in freezerproof ramekin dishes but add an extra egg white when whisking. Thaw at room temperature for 1 hour, then bake as usual.

Flavourings and fillings
• Stir wholegrain mustard, chopped fresh chives and cayenne pepper into a cheese soufflé base before you fold in the egg whites.
• Puréed root vegetables, especially parsnips, make a delicious soufflé base if mixed with Indian spices.
• Chopped smoked fish or shellfish such as crabmeat or fresh mussels added to the egg yolk base are excellent in a soufflé.
• Red peppers boiled until soft with several whole cloves of garlic and then puréed and added to the egg yolks and flour with a little paprika and cayenne pepper make a lovely coloured soufflé.
• Sauces can often be very good finishing touches for soufflés – try heated cream with a soft white garlic cheese melted in, a very smooth vegetable purée with added cream, a curried or cheese béchamel sauce with added cream, or a traditional rich hollandaise sauce.
• Put a little sauce such as homemade fresh tomato sauce in the bottom of the prepared dish before adding the soufflé mixture.

Anna del Conte

Frittata

(The Classic Food of Northern Italy)

A frittata is a thick, flat omelette which you cut into wedges and eat warm or at room temperature. Every cook ought to be able to make one. You can eat little wedges of frittata with your apéritifs or serve bigger pieces with a rocket salad on the side to make a neat first course. Frittatas make marvellous picnic food, or two of you could share one for supper with some bread and a bottle of wine. As with any of the great basics, frittatas can accommodate a wide range of ingredients, from the leftover to the luxurious. 'In Tuscany you would add sage or mint,' Anna del Conte tells us, 'in Lombardy onion, in Umbria a black truffle, in Liguria porcini and in Piedmont sweet peppers. You can add other vegetables, such as leftover sautéed courgettes or stewed fennel, or even leftover spaghetti or tagliatelle. They all go to make a delicious frittata.' If you do add vegetables or leftovers to this recipe, cut the number of eggs down to five.

Serves 4

7 large eggs
40g/1¹/₂oz freshly grated Parmesan

salt and freshly ground black pepper
25g/1oz unsalted butter

Break the eggs into a bowl and beat lightly until blended. Add the Parmesan, salt and pepper, remembering not to add too much salt because the cheese is salty. Beat again.

Melt the butter in a heavy-based 30cm/12 inch frying pan and, as soon as the butter has melted, pour in the egg mixture. Turn the heat down to very low. When the eggs have set and only the top surface is still runny, pass the pan under a preheated grill, just for 30 seconds, enough to set the top.

Loosen the frittata with a spatula and cut into lovely wedges. Transfer to a serving dish or individual plates.

Lesley Chamberlain

Blini

(The Food and Cooking of Russia)

One blini is a *blin*, and not enough – although be aware that if you eat them as a first course you may never get to your second course because you don't eat blini, you overeat blini. Traditional blini can be slightly crumpet-like, so Lesley Chamberlain has come up with *gurevskie blini*, a recipe using baking powder, which gives a lighter, softer pancake, more like a crêpe in fact. If you want to roll your blini around the filling this is the recipe to use, but I must say that I prefer the slightly more leaden originals.

Blini make an excellent first course or light supper served with smoked salmon, caviar (either the real thing or salmon roe, but never lumpfish) or chopped herring, as Lesley Chamberlain suggests. I like the bitterness of buckwheat but it is an acquired taste and you may wish to tone down its flavour a bit by mixing it with white flour. Incidentally, buckwheat is not really wheat at all, but it behaves like a cereal even though it is more closely related to rhubarb.

Easy-blend yeast is probably your best bet if you are making the yeasted blini. One sachet will handle up to 750g/1lb 10oz flour and, unlike fresh yeast or dried yeast granules, you won't end up with that rather acrid taste if you use too much of it.

A Traditional Recipe for Blini

300ml/^{1}/$_2$ pint water and another 100ml/3^1/$_2$fl
  oz milk or water
2 teaspoons dried yeast
sugar to taste
350g/12oz buckwheat flour
^{1}/$_2$ teaspoon salt
1 egg
whipped cream to taste (optional)
butter or butter and oil

Warm the water and milk slightly and dissolve the yeast and sugar in it. When the mixture begins to foam and bubble slightly add it to half the flour, stirring with a wooden spoon to keep it smooth. Leave to rise for 1–2 hours in a warm place, covered with a tea towel or inside a plastic bag. Add the salt, the egg yolk and the rest of the flour, beating well. Leave to rise again for another 1–2 hours. Just before cooking fold in the stiffly beaten egg white and a spoonful of whipped cream for extra lightness and crumbliness. The mixture before cooking may be quite thick.

For cooking use a small, heavy-bottomed frying pan and heat it gently for a few minutes before you are ready to start. Use butter or butter and oil, and reckon, especially the first time, to throw away the first few pancakes until you get the heat and the

amount of fat and batter just right. 'The first pancake turns out a mess' is an old and true Russian saying. Cook for about 4 minutes each side, turning with a spatula. Blini do not toss. A 10cm (4 inch) pan will need about 2 tablespoons of mixture, depending on its thickness, for each pancake. Re-oil the pan after each one is cooked. If you have a set of blini pans they may also be slipped into a hot oven to cook, which was the original method. The mixture makes about 12 blini, which are probably best eaten with chopped hard-boiled eggs and soured cream and/or melted butter. Like English crumpets, they are also excellent just with butter and may be kept warm in the oven. Chopped herring and soured cream is another traditional accompaniment.

Gurevskie Blini

1 teaspoon baking powder	2 eggs
350g/12oz white flour	sour or fresh milk
100g/4oz buckwheat flour	4 tablespoons melted butter
salt	

Sift together the baking powder, the flours and a pinch of salt and add the egg yolks one at a time, stirring with a wooden spoon. Gradually add the warmed milk and melted butter until the mixture has the texture of heavy cream. Beat the egg whites stiffly and add just before cooking. Serve straight from the pan with any of the following:

Finely chopped herring and lemon
Any smoked fish in thin slices, with lemon and butter
Soured cream
Lumpfish caviare and soured cream or lemon and butter
Very finely chopped onion, cooked beetroot and cucumber in French dressing with
    plenty of sugar.

Pasta, Polenta, Rice and Pizza

Pasta with Aubergines

Pasticcio Macaronia

Tagliolini Gratinati al Prosciutto

Egg Noodles with Tofu

Pasta con la Mollica

Polenta

Risotto Parmigiano

Addas Polow

Kedgeree

Riz Arménien

Pizza Rustica

Pizza with Shrimp and Sun-dried Tomatoes

Carla Camporesi
Pasta with Aubergines

(Un Boccone Insieme)

When I travel I like to buy local cookbooks that are the productions of small publishers or enthusiastic amateurs and haven't been picked up by the international publishing network. They make nice souvenirs but can sometimes end up among the least used books in your kitchen. One of the greatest exceptions is the charming and always useful *Un Boccone Insieme* – 'a casual invitation' – printed in both English and Italian, which I bought one summer in the little bookshop in Piazza Matteotti, in Greve, Tuscany.

Pasta with aubergines is a great, usually Sicilian, dish which Carla Camporesi has lightened up and reinterpreted. Traditionally the aubergine is fried and soaks up a large amount of oil in the process. Instead Carla Camporesi cuts the aubergines (preferably small ones) into cubes and boils them, turning them into something similar to what fashion-conscious chefs call 'aubergine caviar'. Her other master stroke is using generous, if unspecified, amounts of a large selection of herbs in her quick-cooked tomato sauce. She doesn't add cheese to this dish; I do. Try passing around some freshly grated pecorino.

Serves 6

4 fine aubergines
400 grams [14oz] pasta (fusilli)
basil

garlic, parsley, thyme, sage, marjoram, wild
marjoram (all chopped)
2 fine ripe tomatoes

Cut the aubergines into medium-sized pieces, but do not peel. Put them on to cook in a large panful of salted water for about 15 minutes, then add the pasta to the aubergines. Whilst these are cooking, take a pan large enough to contain both aubergines and pasta, and gently fry in olive oil the garlic, parsley, basil, thyme, sage and marjorams for several minutes. Add the tomatoes and let simmer for a further 10 minutes. At this stage, the pasta will be ready; add it to the above sauce, together with the aubergines which will have nearly disintegrated, leaving all their flavour.

Pasticcio Macaronia

(The Best Book of Greek Cookery)

Greek food is much maligned. It can be absolutely top class although quite often it isn't. Chrissas Paradissis makes a robust, if not necessarily always convincing, case for the eminence and influence of Greek cooking as follows: the Romans employed Greek cooks, who helped give birth to Italian cuisine, which was then transported to France by Catherine de Medici, bride of the French king, Henri of Navarre, and transmogrified into *haute cuisine*. So, basically, no Greek cooks = no Escoffier. Certainly the Greeks were the most celebrated bakers of Imperial Rome and perhaps their influence filtered into Italian and French cooking.

Pasticcio is one of the world's greatest comfort foods. I first tasted it in a Greek restaurant in Cambridge, Massachusetts, called The Parthenon, which probably introduced more students to the joys of Greek food than any restaurant before or since. Alas, it closed some-time in the Eighties. I still miss it. I used to eat there four or five times a week, having some-how convinced my mother that it was cheaper and easier than cooking in my apartment in Boston.

Chrissas Paradissis's *pasticcio* reminds me of The Parthenon's version. It is a lovely dish to cook – basically little more than a rich meat sauce baked with macaroni and a cheese béchamel. In Greece meat mostly means lamb, and that's what you should use here (although I suppose some health nut in Laguna Beach is making it with minced turkey). Let the filling simmer until it is nice and thick. I don't know what purpose the egg whites serve – I always leave them out. You could use Cheddar for the sauce, but don't. Go and look for some Greek kefalotiri instead. Make this the day before you plan to eat it, if you can. Children love it, too.

Serves 8

1lb [450g] macaroni
1 heaped tablespoon salt
2 heaped tablespoons butter
1 cup [100g/4oz] grated cheese
For the filling:
1 heaped tablespoon butter
2lb [900g] minced meat
1 small onion, chopped finely
1 clove garlic
2 teaspoons salt
½ teaspoon pepper
chopped parsley

½ cup [120ml/4fl oz] white wine
2–3 medium-sized tomatoes, peeled and
   diced, or 1 can (1lb [450g]) tomatoes
2 egg whites
For the sauce:
½ cup [100g/4oz] butter
¾ cup [75g/3oz] flour
4 cups [900ml/1½ pints] hot milk
salt and pepper
nutmeg (optional)
1 cup [100g/4oz] grated cheese
2 eggs and 2 egg yolks

For the filling: heat the butter in a large frying pan and sauté the minced meat and onion until slightly browned. Add remaining ingredients, except egg whites, cover and cook over a medium heat; allow to cool and add egg whites.

To make the sauce: melt butter in a heavy saucepan, add the flour and cook stirring constantly for 1 minute. Add the milk all at once, and stir until the sauce is smooth. Add salt, pepper and nutmeg. Remove from heat and stir in the cheese, eggs and egg yolks.

Cook the macaroni in salted boiling water until soft but firm. Drain and return to the pan. Add the butter.

Butter a 10 x 14 x 2 inch [*25 x 35 x 5cm*] baking pan and put in half the macaroni. Sprinkle with cheese and cover with the meat filling. Top with remaining macaroni. Sprinkle with cheese and cover with the sauce. Sprinkle top with the rest of the cheese and cook in a moderate oven for about 45 minutes or until golden brown. Leave for 20 minutes then cut into square pieces and serve.

Arrigo Cipriani
Tagliolini Gratinati al Prosciutto

(The Harry's Bar Cookbook)

A favourite pastime among those who like eating out is the name-the-best-restaurant-in-the-world game. Of course it's impossible. Anyone's judgement of a restaurant will be influenced by their own state of mind, their companions, the weather and the morning news as much as by the *savoir boire* of the wine steward, the excellence of the chef or the comfort of the banquettes. I don't know what the best restaurant in the world is but if I were to name my three favourites one of them would be Harry's Bar in Venice – a judgement based on over 20 years of sporadic patronage. The first time I went there the Bellinis were the most perfect drinks on heaven and earth, the view across the Grand Canal to Il Redentore was better than any postcard, and the *tagliolini gratinati* just blew my mind. It is, as Cipriani (the owner of Harry's) says, a curious hybrid of a dish: 'The pasta and the ham are Italian; the sauce and the cooking method are French. It has become a classic of Harry's Bar because everybody likes it so much.' The only change that I would make to this recipe is using a full cup (rather than a half) of béchamel sauce.

Serves 6 as a first course or 4 as a main course

salt

3 tablespoons [40g/1½oz] unsalted butter

½ cup [50g/2oz] prosciutto, cut into julienne strips

¾ pound [350g] dried tagliolini or tagliatelle (egg pasta)

½ cup [50g/2oz] freshly grated Parmesan cheese, plus extra to pass at the table

½ cup [120ml/4fl oz] Béchamel Sauce (see below)

Preheat the broiler [*grill*].

Bring a large pot of water to a boil and add a tablespoon of salt.

Melt 1 tablespoon [15g/½oz] of the butter in a large skillet [*frying pan*] over medium-high heat. Add the ham and cook it for a minute or two, stirring constantly. Cook the pasta in the boiling water for 2 minutes or until *al dente*. Drain it well in a colander and put it in the skillet. Toss it with the ham, add another tablespoon [15g/½oz] of the butter, sprinkle with half the Parmesan and toss well.

Spread the pasta evenly in a 2 quart [*2 litre/3½ pint*] casserole. Spoon the sauce over the top and sprinkle with the remaining Parmesan. Cut the remaining butter into bits and scatter over the top. Broil [*grill*] as close as possible to the heat source until golden and bubbly, about 1 to 2 minutes. Serve immediately and pass around a small bowl of grated Parmesan cheese.

Salsa Besciamella
Béchamel Sauce

Makes 2 cups [500ml/17fl oz]

¼ cup [50g/2oz] unsalted butter

¼ cup [50g/2oz] flour

2 cups [500ml/17fl oz] milk

salt

freshly ground white pepper

Melt the butter in the top of a double boiler or in a heavy-bottomed saucepan over low heat. Whisk in the flour and cook gently without browning, stirring constantly, for 4 or 5 minutes. Take the pan off the heat and vigorously whisk in the milk. Cold milk will whisk in smoothly if you do it off the heat. When the sauce is well blended, return it to the stove and cook it over medium heat, stirring constantly, until it is thick and smooth. Use a wooden spoon and be sure to stir in the sauce from the bottom and sides of the pot. Let it come to a boil, then put the pot over simmering water and let it cook gently for another 10 or 15 minutes, stirring frequently. Season the sauce to taste with salt and pepper.

Sri Owen

Egg Noodles with Tofu

(Healthy Thai Cooking)

Tofu – soya bean curd – is not just for ageing hippies and politically correct bunny huggers. It was originally developed as a meat substitute for Chinese Buddhist monks and has been around for at least 700 years. It soaks up flavours well and has an interesting texture, or what food scientists call 'mouth feel' – an inelegant but vivid term. Chinese-style tofu comes packed in water. If you don't use it the day you buy it, change the water, but don't keep it hanging around too long. I prefer buying 'Western' tofu, which is vacuum packed and comes in a number of different flavours. Smoked tofu is especially good. A worthwhile and delicious Oriental technique featured in this recipe is the use of scrambled eggs to enrich the sauce.

Serves 4

225g/8oz dried egg noodles
1/2 teaspoon salt
3 tablespoons groundnut oil
4 shallots, thinly sliced
2 garlic cloves, thinly sliced
1cm/1/2 inch piece of fresh ginger, finely chopped
2 tablespoons light soy sauce

2 fresh tomatoes, peeled and chopped
2 red chillies, deseeded and finely chopped
2 tablespoons yellow bean sauce
200g/7oz block of Chinese-style tofu, cut into 16 cubes
2 eggs, lightly beaten
3 tablespoons chopped spring onions

Cook the noodles: boil 1.2 litres/2 pints water with the salt and add the noodles. While they are boiling, separate them with a large fork so that they cook evenly and don't stick together. Let them boil for 3 minutes, then transfer them to a colander and put them under cold running water until they are cold. Leave them in the colander to drain completely.

Heat half the oil in a wok and stir-fry the shallots, garlic and ginger for 2 minutes. Add the soy sauce and tomatoes and stir for 30 seconds.

Add the cold noodles and keep turning and tossing them around until they are hot again. Remove the wok from the heat and cover it, so that the noodles stay warm.

In another wok or frying pan, heat the remaining oil and add the chopped chillies and yellow bean sauce. Stir these for 2 minutes. Then add the tofu and keep stirring for 2 more minutes. Raise the heat and add the lightly whisked eggs and spring onions. With a wooden spoon, vigorously stir the mixture until the eggs are scrambled.

Transfer the tofu mixture into the warm noodles. Heat together over a low heat, stirring and mixing so that everything is evenly hot. Serve at once.

Valentina Harris

Pasta con la Mollica
Pasta with Breadcrumbs

(Southern Italian Cooking)

This hymn to carbohydrate – pasta with breadcrumbs – sounds decidedly odd, a bit like pasta with potatoes, which is another outstandingly tasty bit of death by starch. It is an exemplar of *cucina povera*, showing how wonderful dishes are often created by the need to use cheap ingredients. What could be more thrifty than topping your pasta with some crumbled stale bread that's been cooked with garlic and olive oil? I am sometimes too lazy to brown the garlic and then remove it from the pan, so I often just soften it in the oil and leave it there. The mixture of garlic, anchovies, tomato and breadcrumbs is powerful, super-savoury and utterly invigorating. It is also excellent poured over some simply grilled fish instead of served with pasta.

It is, of course, absolutely forbidden in the canons of Italian cooking to put grated cheese on any pasta dish made with fish but I happily sprinkle a little grated Parmesan on this one. (I assume the breadcrumbs were originally a substitute for the more expensive Parmesan anyway.) I remember sitting on the terrace of a hotel in Positano and being told by the proprietor that you must really never drink anything but water with pasta. He then paused to pour us each another glass of wine to go with our *spaghetti vongole*. So the rules of Italian cooking are both sacred and made to be broken, reflecting the anarchic streak that permeates Italian culture.

Serves 4

salt
85ml/3fl oz olive oil
2 large cloves garlic, lightly crushed
100g/4oz salted anchovies, rinsed, dried and boned
3 tablespoons chopped fresh parsley

450g/1lb fresh tomatoes, peeled, quartered and seeded
salt and freshly milled black pepper
75g/3oz stale white bread
350g/12oz penne, maccheroni, bucatini or similar-shaped dried durum wheat pasta

Bring a large pan of salted water to a rolling boil for the pasta. Preheat the oven to 230°C/450°F/Gas Mark 8. In a separate saucepan, heat half the oil with the garlic until the garlic is brown. Discard the garlic and add the anchovies. Mash thoroughly into the oil, then stir in the parsley and the tomatoes and season.

Crush the bread into coarse crumbs, then mix with the remaining oil and scatter them all over a baking sheet. Brown in the oven for about 5 minutes, taking care that they do not burn.

Toss the pasta into the boiling water, stir, return to the boil and cook until the pasta is just tender. Drain well and return it to the pan. Pour over the sauce and toss it all together. Transfer into an ovenproof serving dish and scatter with the toasted breadcrumbs. Return to the oven for 2 minutes before serving.

Ruth Rogers and Rose Gray

Polenta

(The River Café Cook Book)

By the time I first visited the River Café in west London – a few months after it opened in 1987 – it was already becoming a well-known secret. It began modestly as the glorified works canteen for the architectural practice of Richard Rogers, known to some as one of the world's greatest architects and to others as the husband of Ruth Rogers. In the often egotistical world of the professional kitchen, the Rogers and Gray partnership is a rare example of a successful double act. The River Café grew quickly from its esoteric beginnings to gain a widely recognized status as one of the best restaurants in a London that now has international credibility as a great restaurant city. Then came the cookbook which, with its typographical cover and black and white photographs, triumphantly broke all the rules to become a major bestseller and fill dinner tables across the land with the River Café's own particular vision of Italian food.

The secret of Ruth Rogers' and Rose Gray's success may lie in their reticent style. Both as cooks and recipe writers they let the ingredients speak loudly. Nothing exemplifies their stature as queens of the neo-peasant food revolution more than the fact that they've turned the London glitterati into a tribe of polenta eaters. Polenta has now almost become the mashed potatoes of the middle classes. Like many staple foods, its preparation is steeped in superstition and ritual. In fact it is really quite easy to cook, although it does tend to splutter and splash rather violently. Incidentally Rogers and Gray are amongst the few recipe writers who recommend specific brands of their ingredients, which is actually rather useful. For making polenta they recommend Bramata polenta flour, which is an organic blend of three different types of corn kernels.

Serve wet polenta as an accompaniment to meat or fish, as you would mashed potatoes. Rogers' and Gray's suggestions for grilled polenta include serving it with San Daniele ham; asparagus and shaved Parmesan; rocket and red chilli; and anchovies, rosemary and lemon. As you will have guessed by now, polenta makes a good 'carrier' for all sorts of forthright flavours. But it is by no means a neutral taste. It really does enhance any ingredient it is served with.

Polenta

Serves 6–8

350g/12oz polenta flour
1.75–2 litres/3–3½ pints water
sea salt and freshly ground black pepper

150g/5oz butter, at room temperature
200g/7oz Parmesan, freshly grated

Put the polenta flour in a jug with a ladle so that it can be poured in a steady stream.

Bring the water to a boil in a large saucepan and add 1 teaspoon of salt. Lower the heat to a simmer and slowly add the polenta flour, stirring with a whisk until completely blended. It will now start to bubble volcanically. Reduce the heat to as low as possible, and cook the polenta, stirring from time to time with a wooden spoon to prevent a skin forming on the top, for about 40–45 minutes. The polenta is cooked when it falls away from the sides of the pan and has become very dense and thick.

Stir in the butter and Parmesan and season generously with salt and pepper.

Polenta alla Griglia

Serves 6–8

Make the polenta as described above, omitting the butter and Parmesan. When ready, transfer to a large flat baking tray or plate, and spread out to form a cake about 2cm/3/4 inch thick. Leave until completely cold, then cut into wedges or slices.

Preheat a grill to very hot. Brush the pieces of polenta on both sides with olive oil and grill for 3 minutes on each side or until crisp and brown.

Arrigo Cipriani

Risotto Parmigiano

(The Harry's Bar Cookbook)

Any Northern Italian who cares about food – that is to say, any Northern Italian – has strong opinions about risotto. When a Venetian friend and I were talking about a well-known Italian cook my friend said that the cook in question was very nice indeed and could be quite knowledgeable but was sadly the sort of person who cooked risotto with a metal spoon. You see, only a wooden spoon will do. Most of us have been told to buy Arborio rice for risotto but Cipriani says no, and suggests you use either Vialone Nano or Carnaroli. 'Both of these varieties cook more evenly than Arborio,' he explains, 'and since they contain more gluten they maintain their strength longer. As the rice cooks, the gluten dissolves, and this allows the grains to cling to each other. The cooked rice has the characteristic texture of risotto – soft but never gummy.'

What makes Cipriani's cookbook so outstanding is this combination of great recipes and a tremendous amount of kitchen lore and knowledgeable chat about ingredients. When you master this risotto recipe you will have added something very important to your culinary repertoire because I can't think of any other recipe that is so basic yet requires such singleminded attention to quality and detail. To quote Cipriani again, 'This is the simplest risotto – there is nothing extra to hide a mediocre rice, a bad butter, or a tasteless Parmigiano. Everything has to be perfect.'

Serves 6 as a first course

5 to 6 cups [*1.2–1.5 litres/2–2¹/₂ pints*] chicken stock, preferably homemade
1 tablespoon olive oil
1 small onion, minced
1¹/₂ cups [*275g/10oz*] short-grain Italian rice, preferably Vialone or Carnaroli

3 tablespoons [*40g/1¹/₂oz*] unsalted butter at room temperature
²/₃ cup [*75g/3oz*] freshly grated Parmesan cheese, plus extra to pass at the table
salt
freshly ground pepper

Bring the stock to a simmer in a saucepan and keep it at a bare simmer.

Heat the olive oil in a heavy-bottomed 3 quart [*2.75 litre/5 pint*] saucepan and cook the onion over medium heat, stirring until the onion is golden but not brown, about 3 to 5 minutes. Add the rice and stir with a wooden spoon to coat the rice well with the oil and onion. Turn the heat to medium-high, add about ¹/₂ cup [*120ml/4fl oz*] of the simmering stock, and keep the mixture boiling, stirring constantly. As soon as the stock has been absorbed, add another ¹/₂ cup [*120ml/4fl oz*] of stock and stir until it is absorbed. You may have to adjust the heat from time to time – the risotto has to keep boiling, but it must not stick to the pot. If your risotto tends to stick, put the pot on a Flame Tamer [*heat diffusion mat*]. Continue adding stock about ¹/₂ cup [*120ml/4fl oz*] at a time, stirring constantly and waiting until each portion is absorbed before adding the next, until the rice is creamy and tender on the outside with each grain still distinct and firm. This will take at least 20 minutes, maybe as long as 30 minutes, depending on your pot and your stove. If the rice is still a bit hard in the middle after you have used all but a few tablespoons of the stock, add boiling water ¹/₄ cup [*60ml/2fl oz*] at a time, stirring it in as you did the stock, until each grain of rice is tender but still has the slightest bit of firmness and the mixture is creamy.

Remove the pan from the heat and vigorously stir in the butter and the Parmesan. This stirring will make the risotto even creamier. Taste and season with salt and pepper. While continuing to stir vigorously, add the few remaining tablespoons of hot stock (or boiling water if you've used all the stock) to make the consistency softer and softer. In Italy we call it *all'onda* – like a wave. Taste carefully for seasoning and serve immediately, passing a small bowl of grated Parmesan cheese.

Margaret Shaida

Addas Polow
Rice with Lentils

(Legendary Cuisine of Persia)

Persian, or Iranian, cooking is among the least known of all the world's significant cuisines. I suppose this has a lot to do with the fact that few Westerners travel to Iran, although since the deposition of the last Shah in 1979, communities of Iranian political emigrés have flourished in America and Europe with their own markets and restaurants. I love the colour, delicacy and perfumed scent of Persian cooking. Anyone who gets a chance to try it will also be intrigued by the way Persian cooks use the contrasting flavours and textures of fruits, nuts, meat and grain. The Persians are acclaimed as the absolute masters of rice cookery, even by other rice-loving Middle Easterners. They often cook their rice in two stages: a quick blanching in boiling water followed by slow steaming, which makes the grains light, separate and fragrant. This magnificent *polow* combines dates, sultanas and lentils with buttery, saffron-scented rice. Margaret Shaida's recipe from her award-winning book *The Legendary Cuisine of Persia* is much more demanding than your average rice recipe but this vegetarian dish is a showstopper. As she notes in her introduction, Persians feel that lentils 'are good to slow the metabolism and calm a temperamental person'.

The recipe refers to 'liquid saffron', which is saffron that has been ground to a powder and mixed with water, in the Iranian style. Margaret Shaida explains how to make it as follows: 'Ensure that the saffron is completely dry. If you suspect it may not be, then put 20 to 30 pistils in a tiny mortar and place in a warm oven for a few minutes. Add half a dozen grains of sugar and with the pestle (or the back of a teaspoon) crush the saffron and sugar to a fine powder. If using within an hour or two, mix with 4 or 5 teaspoons tepid water and leave to infuse to a deep orange colour. If the ground saffron is mixed with the boiling water it can be kept in a jar for several weeks.'

Serves 4–6

500g/1lb 2oz basmati long grain rice	*For the polow:*
6 tablespoons salt	**100g/4oz green lentils**
120ml/4fl oz vegetable oil	**50g/2oz sultanas**
50g/2oz clarified unsalted butter	**100g/4oz stoned dates**
4 teaspoons liquid saffron	*For the garnish:*
	1 medium onion

Pick over the rice, wash thoroughly in 5 or 6 changes of water and leave to soak in salted water to cover by at least 2.5cm/1 inch for 3 hours.

Pick over the lentils, wash and simmer gently in lightly salted water until tender. Strain and reserve, adding the stock to the water for rice.

Clean the sultanas and soak in a little warm water for 20 minutes. Cut the dates across into two and fry briefly in a little oil.

Bring about 2 litres/3½ pints of water with 3 tablespoons of salt to a rapid boil in a 3.4 litre/6 pint saucepan. Pour off excess water from rice and pour into the fast-bubbling water. Bring back to the boil and boil for 2–3 minutes. After 2 minutes, test to see if rice is ready: the grain should be soft on the outside but still firm in the centre. Strain and rinse with tepid water. Toss rice gently in colander.

Return the rinsed-out saucepan to the heat and add oil and 2–3 tablespoons of water. Heat till sizzling. Sprinkle one layer of rice across the bottom. Then spread about a third of the lentils and sultanas over the rice, then another layer of rice and another layer of lentils and sultanas. Repeat once more, finishing with a layer of rice and building it up into a conical shape. Place the dates to one side on top of the rice to steam.

Poke two or three holes through the rice to the bottom with the handle of a wooden spoon. Wrap the saucepan lid in a clean teacloth and cover pan firmly. Keep on a high heat for 2–3 minutes until the rice is steaming, then reduce heat to low for at least 30 minutes. The rice can be kept warm and fresh on the very lowest heat for a further hour or even longer.

Thinly slice the onion and fry briskly in oil until golden brown and crisp.

Place saucepan of rice on a cold wet surface and leave for a minute or two. While waiting, melt the butter and put aside for garnish. Lightly mix 2 or 3 tablespoons of rice with the liquid saffron in a small bowl; reserve for garnish.

To dish up, gently toss and mix the rice and ingredients and sprinkle lightly on to a warmed dish in a symmetrical mound. The dates may be put all round the dish at the base of the rice. Garnish with the saffron rice and the fried onion, and pour the melted butter all over to give it a sheen.

Finally, remove the crusty bottom and serve on a separate plate.

If you wish, tender pieces of lamb may also be served as an accompaniment.

Michael Smith

Kedgeree

(Fine English Cookery)

It began as *khichri*, an Indian dish of rice and lentils, and somehow got transmogrified into a mixture of rice, fish and hard-boiled eggs. Kedgeree was once a breakfast staple, eaten either first thing in the morning or last thing at night after too many hours of dancing and drinking. This culinary monument to the Raj remains a moveable feast, which you are now more likely to encounter at lunch or supper. You can make kedgeree as simple as anything with just fish, eggs, rice, butter and parsley but I like the way Michael Smith binds it together with creamy mushroom sauce. The tinned salmon appears to be a charming period touch that we could do without, as is the pretty appalling suggestion to mould the rice into a ring. Nowadays we would use fresh salmon, which is so much cheaper and more readily available than it was when this recipe was written. In any case, kedgeree ought to be made with smoked haddock, or maybe half salmon and half smoked haddock. Don't be as timid as Michael Smith with the curry powder as, English as this dish has become, it doesn't work unless it pays homage to its Indian ancestry. You might indeed add a further Indian inflection to it by garnishing the finished dish with some onion rings fried until golden brown and crisp.

Serves 4

4 eggs	225g/8oz tin middle-cut salmon (or
175g/6oz rice	350g/12oz piece cooked fresh salmon or
1 small onion	smoked haddock)
100g/4oz button mushrooms	juice of $1/2$ a lemon
50g/2oz butter	fresh parsley
25g/1oz plain flour	150ml/$1/4$ pint single cream (optional – see
tip of a teaspoon curry powder	method)
$1/2$ stock cube	salt and freshly ground pepper
600ml/1 pint milk	

Boil the eggs for no more than 10 minutes from cold (they should still have 5mm/$1/4$ inch of soft centre). Run them under cold water until they are quite cold and then shell them. Cut them into quarters and then into eighths. Cover with foil until you require them.

Cook the rice in plenty of boiling light-salted water for 17 minutes exactly, then run it under the cold tap and wash off the starch. Leave to drain in a sieve or colander.

Finely slice the onion and mushrooms.

Melt the butter in a pan which will be large enough to contain all the ingredients. Add the sliced onion and fry until golden brown, then add the mushrooms and fry for a few seconds before stirring in the flour.

Add the touch of curry powder and the piece of stock cube. Gradually work in the cold milk a little at a time until you have a smooth sauce and simmer for 5 minutes, stirring to ensure that it doesn't stick or burn.

If using tinned salmon, pour the juices from the tin into the sauce. Correct the seasoning and add lemon juice to acidulate lightly. Skin and flake the fish and fold into the sauce, then fold in the cooked rice and gently allow this to heat through, stirring with a 'folding' action as you do so, so that you do not break up the fish too much.

Finally, just before you are ready to serve the kedgeree, carefully fold in the eggs. Pour the kedgeree into a heated dish, sprinkle with parsley and serve.

If the finished dish is too solid for you, add the single cream brought to the boil.

I sometimes serve the rice separately, as it is possible to make it look more attractive this way, particularly if you mould the rice in a buttered ring-mould first, then fill the centre with the salmon (or haddock), eggs and mushrooms in their creamy sauce.

Pierre Franey

Riz Arménien

(More 60-Minute Gourmet)

I'm not totally sure why this is called Armenian rice, as this cooking method is found in various places across the Middle East. The browned noodles add a delicious nutty flavour and a different texture. Anyone can cook this but you must pay attention to the noodle-browning phase, as you want them to be well browned but nowhere near the verge of burned. Pierre Franey recommends using fine egg noodles, which I think is rather too genteel. I use any old bits of pasta that get broken and collect in the bottoms and corners of pasta packets, jars and boxes. Thin pasta works better than fat so, if you can, use short lengths of spaghetti, spaghet-tini, vermicelli or fedellini. You could substitute 1 tablespoon of finely chopped shallots for the garlic – I think it tastes better. It's very nice to cook rice in chicken stock but if you are a vegetarian, or can't be bothered, just use water. You are never ever meant to disturb rice while it is cooking but if, towards the end, you need to add a little more liquid it will hardly be the end of the world. Armenian rice is excellent with grilled chicken or fish or with lamb kebabs. The greedy will take any leftovers the next day, flatten them into little cakes and fry gently in some butter.

Serves 4

1 tablespoon peanut, vegetable or corn oil
¹/₄ cup [*25g/1oz*] fine egg noodles
1 cup [*200g/7oz*] raw rice
1 teaspoon finely chopped garlic

salt and freshly ground pepper
2 tablespoons [*25g/1oz*] butter
1¹/₂ cups [*350ml/12fl oz*] chicken broth
¹/₄ cup [*2 tablespoons*] finely chopped parsley

Heat the oil in a saucepan and add the noodles. Cook, stirring, until browned.
   Add the rice and garlic and stir. Add salt and pepper to taste, butter and the broth.
   Cover and cook over low heat exactly 17 minutes. Stir in the finely chopped parsley and serve.

Pizza Rustica

(Southern Italian Cooking)

People of my generation will first think of Valentina as the ex-wife of Bob Harris, inimitable post-hippie DJ and one-time host of a 'progressive' (e.g. Hawkwind) TV music show called *The Old Grey Whistle Test*. I still often use a well-worn copy of Valentina's first book, *Perfect Pasta*, which, to me at least, immediately established her as a cookery writer to trust. She is also an excellent teacher and an ebullient performer in the kitchen.

This pie is not a conventional pizza and is a lot more interesting than most flans or quiches. Because of the high proportion of eggs, the pastry doesn't get very crispy. The filling is a bit of a moveable feast: you could substitute some bacon for the ham or you could make a vegetarian version with some diced black olives to stand in for the ham's saltiness. Valentina suggests serving it for picnics, which I would go along with provided you can keep it warm *en route:* cold, cooked mozzarella is a bit of a rubbery mess. Why not have it for supper at home instead?

Serves 6–8

extra butter for greasing
extra flour for dusting
For the pastry:
275g/10oz plain white flour
100g/4oz butter, cubed
2 eggs
1 egg yolk

salt
For the filling:
200g/7oz cooked ham, chopped
300g/10oz mozzarella cheese, sliced
2 eggs, beaten
4 tablespoons freshly grated Parmesan
  cheese

Preheat the oven to 220°C/425°F/Gas Mark 7.

Make the pastry first. Pile all the flour on the worktop and make a hollow in the centre with your fist. Put the cubed butter, the eggs and the egg yolk into the hollow. Add a pinch of salt and knead everything together until you have a smooth, soft ball of dough. Divide the pastry roughly in half. Roll out the larger piece on to a floured surface until it is big enough to line a buttered 28cm/11 inch quiche dish. Prick the pastry all over the bottom with a fork. Roll out the second piece of dough until it is big enough to make a lid for the pie.

Scatter the ham all over the bottom of the pastry case. Scatter the mozzarella over the ham. Pour most of the beaten eggs over the ham and mozzarella, reserving a little bit to brush over the finished pie. Sprinkle the grated Parmesan all over and finally place the second piece of pastry dough on top of the filling.

Seal the edges very carefully by pinching them together, then brush the remaining egg all over the lid. Bake for about 25 minutes, or until golden brown. Serve just warm but not too hot.

Wolfgang Puck

Pizza with Shrimp and Sun-dried Tomatoes

(The Wolfgang Puck Cookbook)

Alongside Arnold Schwarzenegger, Wolfgang Puck is Mittel Europ's most successful export to America – or perhaps I should say Hollywood, which is of course a virtual country in its own right. Like tens of thousands of others I have stood in line at Puck's flagship restaurant, Spago – a relatively unassuming joint on Sunset Boulevard – and waited patiently for my lucky number to come up in the form of a table while Bruce and Clint and Demi and Arnold have been whisked past, leaving us nobodies and visiting hayseeds from the sticks shifting hungrily from foot to foot. And, like many others, I have asked myself, why am I waiting here so uncomfortably for so long in order to eat an extremely expensive pizza cooked by some guy who probably knows more about yodelling than *marinara*? The answer, as always, is in the eating. Yes, Wolfgang is a great performer, packager, promoter and salesman but most of all he is a really good cook, with the wit to reinvent a dish that almost everyone likes.

You can make the dough in a food processor, with an electric mixer or by hand. Some cooks find kneading the dough by hand therapeutic, and the warmth of your hands will help the dough to rise. If you are in a particularly bad mood and really take it out on your dough you will get an even better rise. Alternatively you could forgo the whole operation by making your pizza base from a packet of ciabatta bread mix, which you can customize with a bit of extra olive oil.

In Wolfgang's wake, no pizza topping is too outlandish – for example, Peking duck or chicken tandoori – but the master himself has always been pretty circumspect about looking for clear, sharp flavours to put on his pizzas. Shrimp and sun-dried tomatoes is vintage Wolfgang. British cooks can use frozen North Atlantic prawns and you could also substitute some smoked garlic for the blanched garlic in the recipe. Use sun-dried tomatoes that have been packed in oil or rehydrate some of the very dry ones in boiling water. Light sleepers should note that cheese and shellfish combinations are not conducive to dream-free nights.

Makes 4 pizzas

1 recipe Pizza Dough (see below), divided into
    4 equal pieces
2 tablespoons chilli oil
1 cup [*100g/4oz*] grated Italian fontina cheese
2 cups [*225g/8oz*] grated mozzarella or an
    equal amount sliced fresh mozzarella
¹/₄ cup [*4 tablespoons*] blanched garlic,
    chopped

1 medium red onion, thinly sliced
¹/₄ cup [*4 tablespoons*] chopped fresh basil,
    plus 4 small sprigs for garnish
20 to 24 medium shrimp [*prawns*], peeled
¹/₄ cup [*4 tablespoons*] sun-dried tomatoes,
    thinly sliced

Before you are ready to bake the pizzas, preheat the oven with a pizza stone inside to 500°F [*250°C/Gas Mark 10*] for 30 minutes.

Roll or stretch the dough, a quarter at a time, into a 7–8 inch [*18–20cm*] circle and place it on a lightly floured wooden peel.

For each pizza, brush the dough with chilli oil. Top it with a quarter of the fontina and mozzarella, leaving a ¹/₂ inch [*1cm*] border along the edge. Top the cheese evenly with a quarter of the garlic, red onion, basil, shrimp and tomatoes. Assemble the 3 remaining pizzas in the same way.

Slide the pizza on to the hot stone and bake it for 10 to 12 minutes, or until the cheese is bubbling.

Presentation: slide the pizzas on to warm plates, garnish with basil sprigs and serve immediately. Cut into wedges to eat.

Pizza Dough

Makes four 7–8 inch [*18–20cm*] pizzas

3 cups [*350g/12oz*] all-purpose [*plain*] flour
1 teaspoon salt
1 tablespoon honey
2 tablespoons olive oil

³/₄ cup [*175ml/6fl oz*] cool water
1 package fresh or dry yeast
¹/₄ cup [*4 tablespoons*] warm water

Place the flour in a food processor. Combine the salt, honey, olive oil and cool water in a small bowl or measuring cup. Mix well.

Dissolve the yeast in the warm water and let prove for 10 minutes.

With the motor running, slowly pour the salt and honey liquid through the feed tube. Then pour in the dissolved yeast. Process until the dough forms a ball on the blade. If it is sticky, add sprinklings of flour.

Transfer the dough to a lightly floured surface and knead until it is smooth. Place in a buttered bowl and allow the dough to rest, covered, for 30 minutes.

Divide the dough into 4 equal parts. Roll each piece into a smooth, tight ball. Place on a flat sheet or dish, cover with a damp towel and refrigerate.

One hour before baking, remove the dough from the refrigerator and let it come to room temperature.

Lightly flour a work surface. Using the fleshy part of your fingertips, flatten each ball of dough into a circle, about 6 inches [*15cm*] in diameter, making the outer edge thicker than the centre. Turn the dough over and repeat. Lift the dough from the work surface and gently stretch the edges, working clockwise to form a 7–8 inch [*18–20cm*] circle. Repeat with the other 3 pieces. Place the circles on a wooden peel or on baking sheets, and build the pizzas as desired.

Notes

To make the dough in an electric mixer fitted with a dough hook, place the flour in the bowl and add the ingredients in the same order as when using a food processor. Knead the dough in the machine until it forms a smooth ball. Place the dough in a buttered bowl and allow it to rest, covered, for 30 minutes.

To prepare by hand, place the flour on a work surface and make a well in the centre. Add the wet ingredients and proved yeast. Slowly incorporate the flour into the wet ingredients working from the centre outward. When a dough forms, knead it on a floured surface until smooth. Place in a buttered bowl and allow the dough to rest, covered, for 30 minutes.

You can also roll out the pizzas with a rolling pin, then pinch up the edges with your fingers to form a little ridge.

Salads and Vegetables

Valentina Harris

Insalata Arriganata
Potato and Olive Salad

(Southern Italian Cooking)

There are really only two ways to make potato salad: either dress cold potatoes in mayonnaise or toss hot ones in a vinaigrette and let them absorb it. Way number one can be an absolute mess or you can make it the way my mother did, with peeled potatoes, homemade mayonnaise (or decent storebought, thinned with a little cream and a squirt of lemon juice), chopped hard-boiled egg, diced spring onions and plenty of black pepper. It is excellent for picnics and barbecues and particularly nice with either demotic hot dogs or lordly lobster. Way number two, as elucidated by Valentina Harris, is rather less picnicky but wonderful with cold salmon or a nice piece of freshly grilled tuna. Waxy potatoes are always best for salads. Mint marries successfully and frequently with garlic in Italian cooking and makes a nice addition to this dish. Six cloves of garlic sounds like a lot but it's only one per person. Dried oregano works better than fresh here and in many other Italian recipes. If you don't like olives you can always leave them out; the salad works perfectly well without them.

Like most of Valentina's recipes this is straightforward, easy to make and packs a punch. Her style is economical; her flavours aren't.

Serves 4–6

8–10 potatoes, well scrubbed
salt
50g/2oz black olives, stoned and sliced in half
20 leaves fresh mint, chopped

3 tablespoons salted capers, well rinsed, dried and chopped
6 cloves garlic, chopped
12 tablespoons olive oil
1 tablespoon dried oregano

Boil the potatoes in salted water until tender. Drain, cool slightly and then slice them.

Place the potato slices in a salad bowl. Sprinkle with the chopped olives, mint, capers, garlic, oil and oregano. Mix everything together, taste to check for seasoning and leave to stand for about 10 minutes. Toss once again and serve.

Jacques Médecin

La (Vraie) Salade Niçoise
(Genuine) Salade Niçoise

(Cuisine Niçoise)

Too often sloppy cooks use the *salade niçoise* as a fridge-clearing exercise. I have been served *niçoises* full of horrors like niblets, bacon bits and tinned peas. While the Caesar salad (see pages 72–3) takes kindly to innovations, the *niçoise* is altogether more conservative. Unsurprising, then, that this rather prescriptive recipe should come from the pen of 'King' Jacques Médecin, ultra-right-wing mayor of Nice for twenty-four years and obsessive guardian of *niçoise* values. You may think that a *salade niçoise* must contain cooked French beans and potatoes. Médecin says a firm '*non*'. Indeed, the traditional *niçoise* contains neither cooked vegetables nor lettuce and rests instead on a foundation of tender broad beans or artichokes. If you follow the Médecin recipe you must use only the youngest and freshest vegetables, other-wise you might as well travel the cooked bean and potato route. Tuna and anchovies add to the vexed issue. Some fashionable chefs use seared fresh tuna or, even worse, fresh anchovies. They bring nothing to the party but added fuss and expense. Use tinned anchovies and tinned tuna, as this recipe demands. The English novelist Graham Greene, who retired to Nice, was a bitter critic of King Jacques' reign. Indeed, Médecin's recipes are far better than his ethics. In the 1980s he systematically defrauded the Nice opera company of two million francs, which he siphoned into foreign bank accounts. He fled France, first to Japan and then to Uruguay. After a brief spell as a T-shirt salesman there he was extradited back to France, tried, and sentenced to two years in prison.

Serves 6

10 medium tomatoes

3 hard-boiled eggs

12 anchovy fillets or 350g/12oz tinned tunny fish

1 large cucumber

2 green peppers

6 spring onions

225g/8oz small broad beans or 12 small globe artichokes (depending on the time of year, either one or the other, or neither, but not both)

1 clove garlic, peeled and cut in half

100g/4oz black olives

6 tablespoons olive oil

6 basil leaves

salt, pepper

Quarter the tomatoes and salt them slightly on the chopping board. Quarter or slice the hard-boiled eggs. Cut each anchovy fillet into 3 or 4 pieces, or shred the tunny fish. Peel the cucumber and slice finely. Cut the peppers, onions and artichokes or broad beans into very thin slices.

Rub a large salad bowl thoroughly with the two halves of the clove of garlic, put in all the above ingredients except the tomatoes, and add the olives.

Drain the tomatoes, salt them again slightly, and add to the bowl.

Make a dressing with the olive oil, the finely chopped basil, pepper and salt. Pour on to the salad, which should be chilled before serving.

As the various ingredients that go into *salade niçoise* are of bright and contrasting colours, they can be arranged most decoratively in the salad bowl.

Oriental Salad

(Roast Chicken and Other Stories)

Simon Hopkinson and Lindsey Bareham are one of the best teams of cookbook writers. Lindsey used to be the punchy restaurant critic of the London listings magazine *Time Out* and has written a number of engaging books including *In Praise of the Potato*. Simon is a chef steeped in the great traditions of French bistro cooking, which he boldly interpreted and presented at two London restaurants, Hilaire and then the much-lauded Bibendum. Their book *Roast Chicken and Other Stories* is full of good sense and seductive flavours. Oriental Salad is Simon Hopkinson's version of those Thai salads that mix large amounts of cooling herbs with enough chilli to keep you focused. The best way to get very thin slices of carrot and cucumber is with a swivel peeler. As Simon suggests, this is either a good first course or an accompaniment to a main course. It is very good indeed alongside something simple like grilled fish, seared scallops or chicken burgers.

Serves 4

1 small packet rice noodles, cooked as per instructions, drained, rinsed and cooled

225g/8oz bean sprouts

1 large carrot, peeled and thinly sliced lengthways

1 cucumber, peeled, cut in half lengthways, deseeded, and thinly sliced lengthways

two 2.5cm/1 inch pieces of fresh root ginger, peeled, sliced and cut into thin strips

a small bunch of coriander, leaves only

6 mint sprigs, leaves only

3 large mild red chillies, deseeded and sliced into thin strips

1 red onion, peeled and sliced into thin rings

For the dressing:

1 tablespoon toasted sesame seeds

2 tablespoons rice vinegar

2 tablespoons soy sauce

4 tablespoons Oriental fish sauce, such as *nam pla*

1 garlic clove, peeled and finely chopped

1 tablespoon sesame oil

6 tablespoons groundnut oil

Mix the sesame seeds, vinegar, soy sauce, fish sauce and garlic together in a bowl. Whisk in the oils.

In another large bowl, mix together all the salad ingredients thoroughly with your hands. Pour over the dressing, toss lightly and leave to wilt slightly before serving.

Lee Bailey

A Trio of Tomato Recipes

(Lee Bailey's Tomatoes)

Most people know enough food lore to remember that once upon a time tomatoes were thought to be poisonous. Introduced to Europe from the Americas in the 16th century, they aroused only curiosity and terror. I suppose that if you were presented with an unknown fruit that was bright red, highly acidic and related to the deadly nightshade to boot, you might think twice about eating it. Even the Italians – and Italian gastronomy is almost inconceivable without tomatoes – didn't start eating them until the 18th century. Certainly my culinary life would have been impoverished if I had lived back then, as I am an unashamed tomato fanatic – eat them year round, try every variety I can get my hands on, like them raw, cooked, pulped, juiced. The biggest problem for tomatophiles living in Britain is the difficulty in finding good-tasting tomatoes. I cannot bear those bowling-ball-size monstrosities that taste of blockboard and have a lurid pinky tinge. And I do laugh at supermarket tomatoes labelled 'grown for flavour': what are all the other ones grown for then?

As much as I dislike the notion of eating things out of season, and deplore the environmental wastefulness of shipping vegetables around the world, I am hypocritically committed to a year-round supply of tomatoes. Do seek out the best ones you can find, bearing in mind that nothing will ever equal the taste of a home-grown native tomato in season. The best way to enhance the flavour of so-so tomatoes is to follow Lee Bailey's recipe for oven-curing, which is a little more than very slow roasting in as cool an oven as you can muster. My magnificent beast of an oven gets down to a chilly 20°C, and I leave tomatoes to roast in it overnight. Most domestic cookers don't go this low and will roast tomatoes in about 3 or 4 hours. The more slowly you roast them, the more intense the flavour. I like to sprinkle them with a little sugar, which perks them up a bit if I'm not totally convinced about their quality.

Lee Bailey suggests using oven-cured tomatoes in salads. They are dazzling served while still warm with some proper buffalo mozzarella. I eat them like sweeties and also serve them alongside grilled fish or chicken. They're great on pasta, too.

Cornmeal-dusted pan-fried green tomatoes are more than just a curiosity for devotees of the arch-weepy film *Fried Green Tomatoes at the Whistle Stop Café*. Lee Bailey recommends eating them for breakfast; I would also suggest trying them for brunch or as a first-course at dinner.

Finally, the Tomato Sandwiches are more a hymn of praise than a recipe. I have grown up eating what Lee Bailey calls the classic – tomato and mayonnaise on toast – but I have recently been converted to his tomato tea sandwich. Tabasco butter (as many drops of Tabasco as you can take, mixed into softened butter) is an excellent ingredient for many sandwiches. Use a few leaves of rocket if you can't find radish sprouts. And speaking of radishes, one of my favourite-ever sandwiches is thinly sliced radish with salt and pepper on buttered white bread.

Oven-cured Tomatoes

about 3 pounds [*1.5kg*] tomatoes
1 tablespoon minced garlic
1 tablespoon chopped fresh thyme

2 tablespoons olive oil
¼ teaspoon salt
¼ teaspoon black pepper

Core the stem end of the tomatoes and cut an X in the bottom. Dip in boiling water for 8 to 10 seconds, then immediately into ice water. Slip the skins off and cut each tomato in half crosswise.

Line a sheet pan [*baking tin*] with foil and lightly oil it. Place the tomatoes on the foil, cut side down. Combine the remaining ingredients and rub each tomato half with the mixture.

Place in the oven and turn it to 225°F [*110°C/Gas Mark ¼*]. Bake for 5 hours, until the tomatoes are soft but retain their shape. To store, cover with olive oil and refrigerate them.

Cornmeal Pan-fried Green Tomatoes

flour
1 egg beaten with a little milk
yellow cornmeal

¼ inch [*5mm*] slices green tomato
oil for frying
salt and black pepper to taste

Spread the flour on a sheet of waxed paper. Put the egg wash in a shallow dish. Spread the cornmeal on a sheet of waxed paper.

Dredge the tomato slices in flour and shake off the excess. Dip each slice in egg and drain off the excess. Coat with cornmeal, shaking off the excess lightly.

Heat the oil in a large heavy skillet [*frying pan*] over a medium flame. When hot, add the tomatoes. Cook several minutes, until golden, then turn. Sprinkle with salt and pepper.

Tomato Sandwiches

Tomato sandwiches are a snap to make, and if you are not already acquainted with their miraculous curative powers it's time you gave yourself a treat – as well as a treatment.

There are two basic ones: the classic – which is made on nicely toasted bread spread with homemade mayonnaise – and the tomato tea sandwich – which is made on thin-sliced white bread (trimmed) spread with softened Tabasco butter (or plain). Nowadays, I often add a sprinkling of radish sprouts to the tea sandwich.

Of course, there's that great all-American favourite, the BLT, which probably began as the classic and got added to right after the first strip of bacon was fried.

I don't think I have to give you a recipe for making any of these. Luckily, we all seem born with the right instincts.

Julia Child

Caesar Salad

(From Julia Child's Kitchen)

This is as definitive as possible a recipe for the salad that conquered the world. It was invented by an Italian restaurateur, Caesar Cardini, in the seedy Mexican border town of Tijuana in the twenties and then made fashionable by the Hollywood stars and panjandrums who visited there looking for a little *louche* local colour. Julia Child, always the most meticulous of cookery writers, got this recipe from Cardini's daughter. There is no point being *too* dogmatic about what makes a 'real' Caesar salad because, of course, dishes evolve to suit changing tastes. Julia Child is a scholar but nevertheless runs a broad church. However, as she comments in her book *The Way to Cook*, which also features this salad, 'You will hardly be a Caesar enthusiast if you've dined only on restaurant varieties made with cheap oil, store-bought croûtons, garlic powder and old bottled cheese. But what a marvellous salad it is when prepared with fine fresh ingredients.' So crack open that expensive bottle of olive oil and use the best Parmesan you can get – definitely nothing ready grated. One contentious point is the very brief cooking time for the eggs, which doesn't really conform to our current safety standards. If you are worried, either leave them out or boil them for 4 minutes and add the yolks only. Correctly the salad is made without anchovies: the slightly fishy pungency comes from Worcestershire sauce. If you prefer to use anchovies, there is no need to add salt to the salad. Tinned anchovies are best. Salted or marinated ones are a misguided improvement which destroy the complex, finely balanced flavour of the salad.

A worthy innovation that has spread from California is the grilled chicken Caesar. Just add some sliced fillets of chicken breast (preferably marinated in oil and lemon juice before cooking) to the salad as they come hot off the grill.

Serves 4–6

2 large crisp heads Cos lettuce
2 large cloves garlic and a garlic press
salt
175ml/6fl oz best-quality olive oil
50g/2oz plain toasted croûtons (homemade
type of white bread cut into dice and dried
out in the oven)

1 lemon
2 eggs
25g/1oz Parmesan cheese, freshly grated
peppercorns in a grinder
Worcestershire sauce

The Cos lettuce: you want 6 to 8 whole unblemished leaves of Cos, 7.5–18cm/3–8 inches long, per person. Strip the leaves carefully from the stalks, refrigerate rejects in plastic bag and reserve for another salad. Wash your Caesar leaves gently, to keep them from breaking, shake dry, and roll loosely in a clean towel. Refrigerate until serving time.

The croûtons: purée the garlic into a small heavy bowl and mash to a smooth paste with a pestle or spoon, adding ¼ teaspoon of salt and dribbling in 3 tablespoons of the oil. Strain into a medium-sized frying pan and heat to just warm, add the croûtons, toss for about a minute over moderate heat, and turn into a nice serving bowl.

Other preliminaries: shortly before serving, squeeze the lemon into a jug, boil the eggs exactly 1 minute, grate the cheese into another nice little bowl, and arrange all of these on a tray along with the rest of the olive oil, the croûtons, pepper grinder, salt and Worcestershire. Have large dinner plates chilled, arrange the Cos in the largest salad bowl you can find, and you are ready to go.

Mixing the salad: prepare to use large, rather slow dramatic gestures for everything you do, as though you were Caesar himself. First pour 4 tablespoons of oil over the Cos and give the leaves 2 rolling tosses holding salad fork in one hand, spoon in the other; scoop under the leaves at each side of the bowl, bringing the implements around the edge to meet each other opposite you, then scoop them up towards you in a slow roll, bringing the salad leaves over upon themselves like a large wave breaking towards you; this is to prevent them from bruising as you season them. Sprinkle on ¼ teaspoon of salt, 8 grinds of pepper, 2 more spoonfuls of oil, and toss again. Add the lemon juice, 6 drops of Worcestershire, and break in the eggs. Toss twice, sprinkle on the cheese. Toss once, then sprinkle on the croûtons and give 2 final tosses.

Elizabeth David

Mayonnaise

(Summer Cooking)

Elizabeth David has written authoritatively and at great length about mayonnaise at least twice. Her 1960 recipe from *French Provincial Cooking* is full of historical detail and folklore (for example, she reports the legend that it was 'invented by the cook of the Duc de Richelieu in 1756, while the French under his command were besieging the English at Port Mahon in Minorca') and the assertion that 'it is one of the best and most useful sauces in existence'. She then goes on to note that 'because it is not cooked at all the making of it seems to represent to the uninitiated something in the nature of magic'. Because 'it is not cooked at all', many people are nervous about making it these days when the safety of some of our foods has become questionable. If the idea of serving up raw egg yolks unnerves you, read this recipe for instruction and pleasure anyway. I have selected the version Elizabeth David wrote for her 1968 book, *Summer Cooking*. Her variations are useful as well, and you can apply some of them to good-quality storebought mayonnaise if you prefer.

The excellence of a mayonnaise depends upon the quality of the olive oil employed to make it. Use genuine olive oil, heavy but not too fruity, as a mayonnaise always accentuates the flavour of the oil. The more yolks of eggs used the less tricky the mayonnaise is to make, and the quicker. Lemon juice is better than vinegar to flavour mayonnaise, but in either case there should be very little, as the flavour of the oil and the eggs, not the acid of the lemon or vinegar, should predominate.

In France, a little mustard is usually stirred into the eggs before adding the oil; in Italy only eggs and olive oil are used, and sometimes lemon juice.

It is very difficult to give quantities, owing to the difference in weight of different olive oils, and also because mayonnaise is one of those sauces of which people will eat whatever quantity you put before them. For an average amount for 4 people you need the yolks of 2 eggs, about one third of a pint [*200ml*] of olive oil, the juice of a quarter of a lemon or a teaspoonful of tarragon or white wine vinegar, salt.

Break the yolks of the eggs into a mortar or heavy china bowl; if you have time, do this an hour before making the mayonnaise; the eggs will be easier to work; stir in a very little salt, and a teaspoonful of mustard powder if you like it. Stir the eggs for a minute; they quickly acquire thickness; then start adding the oil, drop by drop, and pouring if possible from a small jug or bottle with a lip. Stir all the time, and in a minute or two the mixture will start to acquire the ointment-like appearance of mayonnaise. Add the oil a little faster now, and finally in a slow but steady stream; when half the oil is used up add a squeeze of lemon juice or a drop of vinegar, and go on adding the oil until all is used up; then add a little more lemon juice or vinegar. If the mayonnaise has curdled break another yolk of egg into a clean basin, and add the curdled mixture a spoonful at a time. Well-made mayonnaise will keep, even in hot weather, for several days. If you make enough for two or three days, and it does separate, start again with another egg yolk, as if it had curdled.

Mayonnaise for Potato Salad
Add a little warm water or milk to a mayonnaise made as above, until it is of creamy consistency, easy to mix with the potatoes.

Mayonnaise Mousseuse
Add a teacupful of whipped cream to a plain mayonnaise, but only immediately before serving.

Another way of making this mayonnaise is to fold the stiffly beaten white of one egg into the mayonnaise, also just before serving. Good for cold salmon, and for asparagus.

Horseradish Mayonnaise
Add 1 or 2 tablespoons of freshly grated horseradish (according to how hot you like the sauce) to a cupful of homemade mayonnaise; stir in a little chopped parsley.

Serve with fish and salads.

Sauce Rémoulade
The yolks of 2 hard-boiled eggs, 1 raw yolk, ¼ pint [150ml] of olive oil, a teaspoonful of French mustard, salt, pepper, a teaspoonful of vinegar, tarragon, chives, a teaspoonful of capers.

Pound the hard-boiled yolks to a paste, with a few drops of vinegar. Stir in the raw yolk; add the seasonings and oil as for a mayonnaise; stir in the freshly chopped herbs and capers.

The difference between rémoulade and mayonnaise is in the consistency as well as in the addition of the herbs. The hard-boiled yolks make a rémoulade creamier, not such a solid mass of oil and eggs as a mayonnaise.

Sauce Tartare
Tartare sauce can be made either with an ordinary mayonnaise, or with a rémoulade as above; the additions are parsley, a little very finely chopped lemon peel and a finely chopped gherkin, with a few capers and if possible a little tarragon. The chopped white of an egg can also be added.

Sauce Verte
8 to 10 leaves of spinach, the same number of sprigs of watercress, 3 or 4 branches of tarragon, 3 or 4 sprigs of parsley.

Pick the leaves of the watercress, tarragon and parsley from the stalks. Blanch, with the spinach, in a very little boiling water for 3 minutes. Strain, squeeze quite dry, and pound the herbs in a mortar, then press them through a wire sieve. Stir the resulting purée into a ready-prepared mayonnaise. The herb mixture should not only colour but flavour the mayonnaise, and the tarragon is an important element. This quantity will be sufficient for about ½ pint [*300ml*] of mayonnaise.

For a hot *sauce verte* add the herb mixture to a Hollandaise sauce.

Sauce Ravigote

A big bunch of mixed fresh herbs comprising whatever is available among the following: parsley, chervil, chives, cress, watercress, burnet, thyme, lemon thyme, savory, marjoram, wild marjoram, tarragon. A tablespoon of capers and 2 or 3 anchovy fillets, a yolk of egg, olive oil, vinegar.

Chop the herbs, then pound them in a mortar. Add the chopped anchovies and the capers, a little salt and pepper. Stir in the yolk. Gradually add 2 or 3 tablespoons of olive oil, as for a mayonnaise, then a little vinegar.

There are a good many versions of this sauce, hot as well as cold. This one comes from *La Cuisine Messine* by Auricoste de Lazarque, whose sauces are always just a little better than other people's.

Richard Olney

Gratin de Navets
Turnip Gratin

(Simple French Food)

Turnips are not an Anglo-Saxon taste. Parsnips yes, swedes (which began life as the Swedish turnip) yes, but turnips no. They look, and too often taste, as if they ought to be fed to cattle. This, of course, is sheer prejudice and it is, I must add, such prejudice that makes writing and talking about food so entertaining.

If you think turnips are either pointless or disgusting I implore you to try this recipe. Richard Olney is one of the best exponents of French cooking you can find. I can only describe his style as one of impassioned simplicity.

He will tell you everything you need to know about cooking the dish and nothing else. All you have to do is exactly as he says.

Vegetarians can leave out the ham and the dish will suffer only a little bit. Do not substitute any other cheese for the Gruyère. It is stringy and nutty – good to taste and fun to eat. You could serve the gratin with a green salad as a light lunch or supper dish. It is hard to beat dished up alongside roast lamb or a crisp and golden roast chicken.

Serves 4

garlic
50g/2oz butter (in all)
750g/1¹/₂lb crisp turnips, peeled thickly, sliced thinly, parboiled 2 or 3 minutes, drained
salt, pepper
1 scant teaspoon finely crumbled dried herbs

100g/4oz thinly sliced prosciutto-type ham, cut into a fine julienne
100g/4oz Gruyère, cut into very thin slices
150ml/¹/₄ pint double cream
handful breadcrumbs

Rub well a small gratin dish with garlic (or purée the garlic and rub the dish with the juice, discarding all debris), let dry, butter generously, and arrange the turnip slices, slightly overlapping, in three layers, sprinkling with salt, pepper, herbs and the julienne ham in between the two intermediate layers. Arrange the slices of cheese on the surface, pour over the cream, sprinkle with breadcrumbs, cover with paper-thin shavings of butter. Bake 45 minutes in a 200°C/400°F/Gas Mark 6 oven.

Robin Howe

Spanakopita

(Greek Cooking)

I have mentioned elsewhere in this book my student devotion to the late lamented Parthenon restaurant of Cambridge, Massachusetts. Every Friday, Aristotle the cook would make a huge tray of spanakopita. It is one of those dishes I dream about. Robin Howe's recipe is the closest thing to it that I have ever been able to concoct. She unusually suggests that the spinach should be sprinkled with salt and pepper and allowed to rest for an hour before cooking in order to degorge the bitter juices. It works.

Filo pastry can be rather fiddly. You must be sure to brush it with oil or melted butter and cover the unused sheets with clingfilm or a damp tea towel to keep them from drying out.

Some recipes add a beaten egg to the filling of this pie, which will give a slightly firmer texture.

There is, alas, a lot of dodgy feta on the market made from cow's milk and sold in huge, blindingly white slabs. Get the real thing, made from sheep's milk by a Greek in Greece. It has an altogether nicer flavour – more tangy and less watery. Good feta is quite salty so watch the amount of salt you add to the spinach.

This pie cut into hefty squares is altogether nicer than the little triangles filled with feta and spinach which you may have eaten in Greek or Cypriot restaurants. Serve it hot or cold, as Robin Howe suggests, or tepid as the Greeks do. It is wonderful on a picnic.

900g/2lb spinach
salt and pepper
1 cup olive oil
2–3 large, finely chopped onions

225g/8oz mashed feta cheese
2 tablespoons finely chopped parsley
1 tablespoon finely chopped dill
10 sheets of filo pastry

Thoroughly wash the spinach, chop it finely, sprinkle it with salt and pepper and leave it for 1 hour. Squeeze it to remove its bitter liquid. Heat the olive oil and fry the onions until brown, add the spinach and cook this until tender, stirring all the time. With a perforated spoon take it from the pan and put it into a bowl. Crumble the feta cheese into the bowl, add pepper, parsley and dill. Mix well. Let the olive oil cool.

Brush with oil a 7.5cm/3 inch-deep baking tin – it should be about 30cm/12 inches in length and about 20cm/8 inches wide – and line it with 1 sheet of pastry. Brush this with oil, add 4 more sheets of pastry, brushing each with oil. Cover the last sheet with the spinach mixture, add the remaining pastry, each sheet brushed with oil. Score the top sheet into squares – using a sharp, pointed knife – sprinkle the top lightly with water, to prevent the pastry from curling upwards, and bake the pie in a moderate oven until the top is a golden brown, about 40 minutes. Cool slightly before cutting into squares and serve either hot or cold.

Elizabeth David

Ratatouille

(Mediterranean Food)

There is much interest in the life of the late Elizabeth David and her seductive combination of fashion model and visionary food writer. Her recipes have a telegraphic simplicity and a blunt honesty that few other food writers have equalled. Few people outside Britain can realize the electrifying effect she had on the cooking and psychology of a country exhausted by World War II and still in the grip of food rationing when her first book, *Mediterranean Food*, was published in 1950. To an austere Britain, olive oil and aubergines were siren calls to a languid, sensual life.

Everyone has eaten ratatouille but far too often it is smothered with tinned tomatoes (all right in their place) and mugged by heaps of dried herbs. Elizabeth David's version is altogether cleaner and clearer tasting. Ratatouille is usually served hot or far too cold. Try it at room temperature with some crusty bread, either as a first course or a light supper. It is also delicious alongside a simply grilled fillet of sea bass or some swordfish that has been quickly cooked in a dry frying pan and then dressed with lemon juice and black pepper.

3 or 4 tomatoes	2 red or green pimentos
2 aubergines	oil
2 large onions	salt and pepper

Peel the tomatoes and cut the unpeeled aubergines into squares. Slice the onions and pimentos. Put the onions into a frying pan or sauté pan with plenty of oil, not too hot. When they are getting soft add first the pimentos and aubergines, and, ten minutes later, the tomatoes. The vegetables should not be fried, but stewed in the oil, so simmer in a covered pan for the first 30 minutes, uncovered for the last 10. By this time they should have absorbed most of the oil.

Claudia Roden

Tarte aux Oignons d'Alsace

(The Book of Jewish Food)

Claudia Roden was given this recipe by a reader she met in a Paris library when she was researching her *Book of Jewish Food*. If, like me, you believe that the simplest dishes are often the nearest to perfection, this tart will become part of your cooking repertoire. Think of it as a quiche Lorraine without the ham and cheese.

As in Claudia's pissaladière recipe (see page 22), much depends on cooking the onions patiently and exactly. I like the way the pastry is pressed into the tart tin rather than rolled out. If you are at all clumsy with pastry (and I am) this is a sure-fire, no-tear method. You could add a little nutmeg to the filling.

Serves 6

For the pastry:

120g/4½oz unsalted butter
250g/9oz plain flour
¼ teaspoon salt
1 egg, lightly beaten
1–2 tablespoons milk (if required)

For the filling:

3 large onions, about 750g/1½lb
50g/2oz butter
2 tablespoons sunflower or light vegetable oil
salt
2 tablespoons plain flour
300ml/10fl oz double cream
2 eggs, lightly beaten
white pepper

For the pastry: cut the butter into small pieces and rub it into the flour and salt with your hands. Add the egg, mix well, and work very briefly with your hand until bound into a soft dough, adding a little milk if necessary. Cover in clingfilm and leave in a cool place for 1 hour.

For the filling: cut the onions in half, then into thick slices. Heat the butter with the oil in a large pan and cook the onions over very low heat and with the lid on for about 1 hour, until very soft and lightly coloured, stirring occasionally and adding a little salt. Now add the flour and stir well.

Beat the cream into the eggs. Let the onions cool a little before stirring in the cream mixture. Taste before adding a tiny bit of salt if necessary and pepper. This should not be a salty tart.

Line a greased 25cm/10 inch tart pan or flan mould with the dough by pressing it in with the palm of your hands (easier to do with this soft dough than to roll it out) and pressing it up the sides. Pour in the filling mixture and bake in an oven preheated to 150°C/300°F/Gas Mark 2 for 1 hour, or until set and golden. Serve hot or cold. It is nicer hot.

Anna del Conte

Parmigiana di Melanzane
Baked Aubergines with Mozzarella and Tomato Sauce

(Secrets from an Italian Kitchen)

This is a fabulous version of a tremendously useful dish, perfect for vegetarians and meaty enough for the most demanding carnivores. If you thought it was smart enough (sadly, most people don't), you could even serve it for dinner parties. I must confess that I've never seen the addition of hard-boiled eggs (which you can just as easily leave out) in any other recipe for this dish. Don't be tempted to think you can make this better by cooking it with the high-priced mozzarella made out of water buffalo milk. That stuff's really only for eating raw and is rather too delicate (and a bit too watery) for cooking with. For a little extra excitement, you could add one or two crushed dried red chillies to the tomato sauce.

Serves 4–5

1kg/2¹/₄lb aubergines	1 garlic clove, peeled and squashed
salt	a few basil leaves, torn, or 1 teaspoon oregano
1 Italian mozzarella cheese, finely chopped	freshly ground black pepper
5 tablespoons olive oil	vegetable oil for frying
400g/14oz tinned plum tomatoes without the juice, coarsely chopped	50g/2oz freshly grated Parmesan
	2 hard-boiled eggs

Wash and peel the aubergines and cut them lengthwise in slices about 5mm/¹/₄ inch thick. Sprinkle generously with salt, put in a colander and leave them to drain for 2 hours or longer. Rinse them under cold water and dry properly with kitchen paper.

Grate the mozzarella through the largest holes of a cheese grater, or cut into very small pieces. Put in a bowl, cover with 1 tablespoon of the olive oil and leave to soak for 30 minutes or longer.

Heat the oven to 200°C/400°F/Gas Mark 6.

Put 1 tablespoon of the olive oil in a small saucepan together with the tomatoes, garlic and basil. Add seasonings and cook at a lively simmer for 5 minutes. Purée the sauce through a sieve or a food mill.

Pour enough vegetable oil in a frying pan to come 2.5cm/1 inch up the side of the pan. Heat the oil and when very hot (test it by immersing the corner of an aubergine slice: it should sizzle) put in as many aubergine slices as will fit in a single layer. Fry to a golden brown on both sides (this will take about 5 minutes) and then retrieve them with a slotted spoon and drain on kitchen paper. Repeat until all the aubergine is fried.

Smear the bottom of a shallow ovenproof dish with 1 tablespoon of the olive oil. Cover with a layer of aubergine, spread over a little tomato sauce and some mozzarella. Sprinkle with a lot of freshly milled pepper and with some Parmesan. Spread over a few slices of the hard-boiled egg and then cover with another layer of aubergine. Repeat these layers until all the ingredients are used up, finishing with a layer of aubergine. Pour over the remaining oil and bake in the preheated oven for about 30 minutes.

Claudia Roden

Potato Latkes

(The Book of Jewish Food)

The fashion for rösti − Swiss grated potato pancakes − puzzles me. I do like them, but why cook rösti when you can make latkes instead? There are almost as many recipes for potato cakes as there are European cultures, but I would put latkes at the pinnacle. They are cooked and served by both Christian and Jewish families throughout Poland and Lithuania. This version comes from Claudia Roden's blockbusting *Book of Jewish Food*, which, like her earlier *Book of Middle Eastern Food*, is a magisterial work of great scholarship and good cooking.

You can serve latkes as a first course or a side dish or, as Claudia notes, 'even for tea with a sprinkling of sugar' − although that might be a latke too far. They also make a good main course served with a large dollop of soured cream or apple sauce.

Serves 6

1kg/2¼lb potatoes	**salt**
2 large eggs	**oil for frying**

Peel and finely grate the potatoes. Put them straight into cold water, then drain and squeeze them as dry as you can by pressing them with your hands in a colander. This is to remove the starchy liquid, which could make the latkes soggy.

Beat the eggs lightly with salt, add to the potatoes, and stir well. Film the bottom of a frying pan with oil and heat. Take serving-spoonfuls, or as much as 50ml/2fl oz, of the mixture and drop into the hot oil. Flatten a little, and lower the heat so that the fritters cook through evenly. When one side is brown, turn over and brown the other. Lift out and serve very hot.

Variations
You may add black pepper, chopped parsley and finely chopped onion to the egg and potato mixture.

Adding 4 tablespoons of potato flour binds the fritters into firmer, more compact cakes, easier to handle but not quite as lovely to eat.

Nigel Slater

Roast Potatoes

(Real Cooking)

So many ways to cook potatoes and so little time to try them all. Who could choose which way to cook potatoes for their last supper? In the middle of a sleepless night it is a good culinary means of 'counting sheep'. Many people would choose roast potatoes – something I tried for the first time when I first visited England. Few of the world's dishes reach the heights of the perfect roast potato. Nigel Slater produces the definitive recipe. I can add only a few comments. He shakes the potatoes in the saucepan they are cooked in; I would shake them roughly in a sieve. The object is the same – to give the parboiled spuds rough edges for extra crispness when roasted. Secondly I would underline his instruction that the potatoes must go into hot fat. As an alternative to the traditional fat from the roast, you could try mixing sunflower and olive oils, half and half. Finally, remember that, as Nigel Slater says, the roasting will take 'a good forty-five minutes, *maybe longer*'. My italics. How many impatient cooks driven mad by the sight of still-pale potatoes have ruined them by shoving them under a grill or putting the oven heat up far too high? I confess.

Serves 4

900g/2lb (about 5) large, floury potatoes, such as King Edwards
lard, dripping or fat from the roast

Peel the potatoes. I would love to suggest that you don't have to but they will develop the hide of a rhinoceros. Cut them into a comfortable size (you know how big you like your roast potatoes to be), but not too small. Put them in a saucepan of cold water and bring them to the boil. Add salt, a teaspoon or so, and turn down to a simmer. The water should be at a rolling boil. Give them a good five minutes, probably a bit longer, until they are slightly soft around the edges.

Drain the water off, then return the pan to the heat. Shake the pan so that the edges of the potatoes are slightly scuffed. This will give them wonderfully crunchy, frilly edges. Tip the potatoes into a shallow metal pan in which you have heated the fat, be it lard, dripping or even olive oil. Roll the spuds in the fat, then bake in a preheated oven at 200°C/400°F/Gas Mark 6 until thoroughly golden and crisp. A good forty-five minutes, maybe longer. Move them only once or twice during cooking, otherwise the edges will not crisp and brown.

Tip off any extra fat, sprinkle the potatoes with salt and return them to the oven for a few minutes longer till they are golden brown and crisp. Eat while hot, though it has to be said they are pretty good eaten when almost cold, or even prised away from the roasting tin the next day.

Rick Stein
Spinach with Butter

(Rick Stein's Taste of the Sea)

Rick Stein's cookbooks and television appearances have been so acclaimed that the Cornish port of Padstow where he makes his base has become a major destination for gastro-tourists. He so dominates the local scene that the place is now half-jokingly known as Padstein. Spinach goes well alongside fish and Rick's recipe for spinach is simple and irreproachable, without any of that annoying metallic flavour that spinach can sometimes have.

Serves 4

225g/8oz spinach leaves
25g/1oz unsalted butter
salt and freshly ground black pepper

Pick over the spinach leaves and wash in at least two changes of water. Bring a pan of salted water to the boil, drop in the spinach leaves, bring back to the boil and strain. Give the colander you strain the leaves through a good shake to get as much moisture out of the spinach as possible, then return the leaves to a clean pan with the butter. Cook very gently for about 2 minutes, driving off the steam and concentrating the flavour slightly. Season with salt and pepper.

Irene Kuo

Stir-fried Asparagus

(The Key to Chinese Cooking)

When I was little, my absolute favourite summer supper was a heap of asparagus on toasted brown bread soaked with melted butter. I can't say that 40 years of eating since then has made my taste any more sophisticated. There is still nothing to beat fresh asparagus spears in season and they are honestly not worth eating if they have been bottled, tinned, frozen or air-freighted. You might just as well eat a cricket bat as one of those enormous out-of-season monsters that you see in markets and on the hors d'oeuvre trolleys of pretentious hotels and restaurants.

When you can get good asparagus there are only three ways to cook it: boiled; tossed in olive oil and sea salt and thrown on to a hot ridged cast-iron grill pan; or, maybe best of all, cooked as Irene Kuo recommends, which will make them 'quite simply magnificent in colour, texture and taste'. I like a cook who doesn't hide her light under a bushel. Irene's method is also a terrific way to cook broccoli. By the way, to roll-cut the asparagus you slice each spear on the diagonal, rolling it a quarter-turn towards you between each cut. But don't worry if you just cut them conventionally.

Serves 2–4

1 pound [450g] asparagus
2 tablespoons oil
1/2 teaspoon salt

3/4 cup [175ml/6fl oz] chicken stock or water
2 teaspoons sesame oil

Wash the asparagus under cold water, especially the tips, where sand often lodges within the buds. Snap off the tough ends. Roll-cut the spears into 3/4 inch [2cm] long pieces. Heat a wok or large, heavy skillet [frying pan] over high heat until hot; add the oil, swirl, and heat for 30 seconds. Turn heat to medium high, scatter in the asparagus and stir rapidly to roll them in the hot oil; their colour will brighten vividly. Sprinkle in the salt and stir once or twice; then pour in the stock, cover, and steam-cook vigorously for 5 minutes. Uncover, dribble in the sesame oil, and stir in sweeping motions until the tiny amount of liquid has completely evaporated. Pour into a hot serving dish.

Richard Olney

Gratin Dauphinois

(Simple French Food)

Arguments have raged over what makes an authentic *gratin dauphinois*. Richard Olney's introduction neatly summarizes the contentious nature of this dish: 'Egg and cheese are included in the recipes from old cookbooks (too far removed from the sources, according to the purists). Nearly every reputed restaurant has its celebrated *gratin dauphinois* and each is willing to divulge its recipe, usually incomprehensible and conceived in the interest of mystification.' While some puritans think the gratin assaults the potato with too many other flavours and textures, I find it one of the best treats for the potato mad. The choice of potato is absolutely crucial. British cooks should choose something nice and waxy such as Pentland Javelin, Ulster Sceptre, Maris Piper or Romano. As with everything else you cook, it is important not to compromise on ingredients. A gratin made with the wrong type of potato will be a lousy dish no matter how great your skill or how rich the cream.

You can slice potatoes in a food processor or treat yourself to a mandoline, which is a real hoot to use provided you mind your fingers and knuckles. (If you are the sort of cook who likes a glass of wine in the kitchen, don't drink it until you've put your mandoline away.) The quantity of milk you'll need depends on the size of your dish: about 300ml/½ pint of milk and 150ml/¼ pint of double cream should do the trick. This is not a dish for control freaks as you need to be flexible about the cooking time. It may be longer than Richard Olney's hour. I am tempted to use more garlic than he does and I also like to grate a little nutmeg over the potatoes. For convenience, you can cook the gratin in the morning and reheat it in the evening. I like it best with roasts but it is also surprisingly good with a grilled tuna steak.

Serves 4

2 cloves garlic	**salt**
butter	**milk**
675g/1½lb potatoes, sliced thinly lengthwise on a mandoline	**double cream**

Earthenware will take the garlic better than other materials. Rub a large gratin dish with garlic (or, which is easier and more effective, put the peeled cloves through a garlic press, rubbing the purée and juices all over the sides and bottom of the dish and discarding any solid debris that remains), leave for a few minutes until the garlic juice has completely dried and is no longer tacky to the touch, butter the dish liberally, and pack in the potatoes in lightly salted layers. Pour over enough milk to just cover the potatoes, bring the liquid to a boil on top of the stove (using an asbestos pad to protect earthenware from the direct flame), spread a thin layer of cream over the surface, distribute thin shavings of butter, and bake in a 190°C/375°F/Gas Mark 5 oven for about an hour or until the liquid has been nearly completely absorbed, the potatoes give no resistance to a knife point, and a richly coloured skin has formed on the surface.

Meat, Poultry and Game

Grand Prize Chilli

Yankee Pot Roast

Kalio

Steak Salad

Palak Gosht

Scallion 'Exploded' Lamb

Leg of Lamb Andalusian Style

Pla Moo

Estouffade of Goat

The Epicure's Kidneys

Involtini con Funghi

Honey-roasted Pork

Chicken Fu Yung Sauce for Vegetables

Poulet Sauté

Stir-Fried Chicken with Ginger, Cardamom and Cashew Nuts

Chicken Kdra with Almonds and Chickpeas

Roast Chicken with Lemons

Roast Turkey with Mosaic of Sage

Shichimi-spiced Duck and Escarole Salad with Ginger Vinaigrette

Canard aux Pêches

Codornices Asadas en Mole de Cacahuale

Provençal Rabbit Stew with Olives and Capers

Ray Calhoun

Grand Prize Chilli

(Southwest Tastes)

Kit Carson was one of the most energetic explorers of America's Western frontier in the mid 19th century. His dying words were reputedly, 'I just wish they was time for another bowl of red.' A 'bowl of red' is a helping of chilli, America's greatest contribution to the world's canon of red-hot foods. It is an easy dish to get wrong; some versions are little more than a bit of stewed mince with some kidney beans tossed in for interest. As with other great dishes, debate rages over just what makes real chilli. Should the beef be minced or in chunks? With beans or without? Do you serve it with soured cream or cheese or both? Ray Calhoun's chilli recipe (published in *Southwest Tastes* by Ellen Brown) makes the best bowl of red that I've ever tasted. Calhoun's business is information – he started working for Texas Instruments in 1963 – but his passion is chilli, and he has regularly won the most Olympian chilli-cooking contests. His philosophy is admirable and could be applied to many other dishes: 'The secret to good chilli is to keep it simple. You improve your chilli by removing ingredients from your recipe.' I make two modifications to this recipe. Like many chilli cooks I substitute lager for the water and, because American tomato sauce isn't available in Europe, I use a bottle of Italian passata instead. You can substitute venison for the beef and one of the best Californian cooks I know makes her chilli with turkey.

Serves 8–10

¼ cup [4 *tablespoons*] vegetable oil

3 pounds [*1.5kg*] beef chuck or round, cut into ¼ inch [*5mm*] cubes or 'chilli ground' (very coarsely ground, available in some markets)

1 onion, peeled and finely chopped

4 garlic cloves, peeled and finely chopped

1 tablespoon paprika

5–6 tablespoons chilli powder

1 tablespoon ground cumin

1 teaspoon dried oregano

one 8 ounce [*225g*] can tomato sauce

1 teaspoon salt

1 cup [*250ml/8fl oz*] water or more

1 jalapeño chilli, deseeded and halved, or 1 teaspoon cayenne (optional)

3 cups [*500g/1lb 2oz*] cooked pinto beans

finely minced onion

1 cup [*100g/4oz*] grated Cheddar cheese

In a covered saucepan, heat the oil over medium-high heat and cook the beef until it is evenly browned and no pink shows. Add the onion and garlic and sauté until the onion is translucent, about 5 minutes. Add the paprika, chilli powder, cumin and oregano and stir for 3 minutes to cook the spices. Add the tomato sauce, salt and water and stir to combine. Add the extra chilli or cayenne if you want a hotter chilli.

Bring to a boil and simmer, covered, over low heat for 2 hours, stirring occasionally and adding more water as needed, up to 1 cup [*250ml/8fl oz*] depending on the rate of simmer. To serve, place some pinto beans in the bottom of bowls and ladle in the chilli. Sprinkle with chopped onion and cheese.

Note: The chilli can be made up to 3 days in advance, and it freezes extremely well.

Jasper White

Yankee Pot Roast

(Jasper White's Cooking from New England)

There is a New England saying that goes, 'To a foreigner all Americans are Yankees; to an American all New Englanders are Yankees; to a New Englander anyone from Vermont is a Yankee; but to someone from Vermont only a man who eats apple pie for breakfast is a Yankee.' I have seen people (including my late father) eat apple pie for breakfast in New England and that is as good a mark of a serious New Englander as any. But I would also put forward a devotion to Yankee Pot Roast, which Jasper White describes as 'very special in its cooking method, with no counterpart that I know of. What makes pot roasting different is that it combines braising and roasting.' White's contribution to the evolution of this great classic is a splash of red wine and cutting the vegetables in *bâtonnets*, which gives a slightly fresher, lighter flavour. Chuck is an American cut; topside would be more suitable in the UK. Jasper White suggests a cooking time of 2 hours at 180°C/350°F/Gas Mark 4, I'd go for 3 hours at 170°C/325°F/Gas Mark 3. The resulting dish should be meltingly tender, enhanced by the flavour of all those root vegetables which will have caramelized in the meat juices with gentle overtones of thyme and bay. Drink the same red wine you threw into the pan and try to make it a good one.

Serves 6–8

1 piece of chuck, about 4 pounds [*1.75kg*], with a thin layer of fat on one side
kosher [*sea*] salt and freshly ground black pepper
3 tablespoons oil
6 cloves garlic, finely chopped
1 medium onion, finely chopped
1 medium carrot, finely chopped
2 tablespoons flour
2 cups [*500ml/17fl oz*] water
1 cup [*250ml/8fl oz*] red wine

4 sprigs fresh thyme, leaves only
2 bay leaves
1 pint basket pearl onions [*350g/12oz*]
4 carrots, cut in *bâtonnets* (see Note below)
1 small or ½ large rutabaga [*swede*], cut in *bâtonnets*
4 parsnips, cut in *bâtonnets*
1 large celery root [*celeriac*] or 4 stalks celery, cut in *bâtonnets*
3 tablespoons freshly chopped Italian [*flat-leaf*] parsley

Preheat the oven to 350°F [*180°C/Gas Mark 4*]. Season the meat with salt and pepper. Place a deep, heavy roasting pan on top of the stove over medium heat and add the oil. When the oil is hot, place the roast in the pan, fat side down. After searing the fat side, turn the meat and brown on all sides. Remove from the pan and set aside. Add the chopped garlic, onion and carrot to the pan and cook for 1 minute. Sprinkle the flour over the vegetables and cook for 1 minute more, stirring constantly. Add the water and red wine, a little at a time, allowing the sauce to thicken before adding more. When all the liquid has been added and has come to a boil, add the thyme and bay leaves. Return the meat to the pan. Season the sauce lightly with salt and pepper. Place the pan, uncovered, in the oven.

Cook the pot roast for 2 hours, turning it every 20 to 30 minutes and checking that it is not cooking too hard. The sauce should be bubbling gently. If it seems too thick, add water.

Meanwhile, put the unpeeled pearl onions in a saucepan and cover with cold water. Add 1 teaspoon salt and bring the onions to a boil; simmer for 1 minute, then drain. When the onions are cool enough to handle, peel them without cutting too deeply into the root end, which holds them together. Set aside.

After the roast has cooked 2 hours, add the onions, carrots, rutabaga, parsnips and celery root. Simmer 20 minutes more, stirring at least once during that time. Remove from oven and put on a low heat over the stove.

Carve the pot roast into ½ inch [*1.25cm*] slices and arrange on a platter. Skim the sauce of any excess fat. Season to taste with salt and pepper. Spoon the vegetables and sauce over the meat and sprinkle with chopped parsley.

Note
To make *bâtonnets*, peel the vegetables and cut into pieces 2 inches [*5cm*] long by ³/8 inch [*1cm*] wide (like French fries).

Maureen Suan-Neo

Kalio
Indonesian Braised Beef

(Red Heat)

Maureen Suan-Neo is one of the best Asian cooks in Europe. I first tasted her vivid cooking when she and her husband John ran a little restaurant around the corner from me in London. Today they have a mini empire of Southeast-Asian restaurants in the City, where lucky stockbrokers and commodity traders can take their tastebuds on holiday. As a cook and recipe writer, Maureen has the courage of her convictions and she manages to make Asian recipes comprehensible to Western cooks without any 'dumbing down'. This simple-to-make but complex-tasting braised beef dish comes from Indonesia. As Maureen explains: 'My father was of Indonesian-Chinese origin, another hybrid of Chinese settlers and Indonesian wives. Undoubtedly, my mother's culinary repertoire encompassed recipes from his culinary background.' Given the mixed provenance of this recipe, you shouldn't feel shy about incorporating it into an otherwise Western menu. If you have trouble finding candlenuts you can substitute their better-known cousin, the macadamia. Galangal is a relative of ginger: if you can't find it, leave it out and just add a little more ginger instead. Finally if you are not near an Asian market that sells palm sugar, use soft light-brown sugar.

Serves 4

2 tablespoons cooking oil

450g/1lb braising steak, cut into bite-sized chunks

1 litre/1¾ pints water

1 teaspoon salt

225g/8oz coconut powder dissolved in 1 cup hot water

For the rempah:

2 stalks lemongrass, finely sliced

10 shallots, chopped

6 cloves garlic, chopped

5cm/2 inches ginger, finely sliced

5cm/2 inches galangal, finely sliced

6 large red chillies, finely sliced

10 candlenuts, crushed

4 tablespoons cooking oil

For the powdered ingredients:

1 tablespoon coriander powder

1 teaspoon ground black pepper

4 tablespoons chopped palm sugar

Make *rempah* by blending ingredients to a fine paste in liquidizer using 4 tablespoons of cooking oil to lubricate the blades. Remove from blender and mix in powdered ingredients.

Heat cooking oil in a heavy-based saucepan and fry *rempah* mixture until fragrant and the oil has separated from the mixture. Add beef chunks and stir to coat the pieces evenly with the spice mixture. Top up with the water and simmer on low heat for 45 minutes until beef is tender. Alternatively, reduce the amount of water and bake in a preheated oven for 45–60 minutes, 200°C/400°F/Gas Mark 6. During the last 10 minutes of cooking, add salt and coconut milk. Skim off excess oil before serving.

Meat, Poultry and Game

Pierre Franey

Steak Salad

(More 60-Minute Gourmet)

In the Fifties Pierre Franey was chef at the once-celebrated restaurant Le Pavillon in New York but he is, I think, more worthy of homage as the author of *The 60-Minute Gourmet* and *More 60-Minute Gourmet*. Both books owe some inspiration to the amusing *Cooking in Ten Minutes* by Edouard de Pomiane, but whereas you can cook only a few interesting things in 10 minutes (especially if you like omelettes), you can cook many more in 60.

Warm salads have had their moment of trendiness but they deserve to be part of any cook's standard repertoire. Franey speculates that they derive from Southeast Asian cooking, which I'm prepared to buy. It's important to blanch the vegetables as instructed: blanching preserves their natural colour and leaves them crisp but not raw. Feel free to experiment with the vegetables. You may dislike red or green peppers or, as I do, you may think that life offers more edifying diversions than taking the kernels off an ear of corn. British cooks will not be able to buy shell steak: ask your butcher for skirt instead. You could also very reasonably make this salad with grilled chicken.

Serves 8 or more

3 shell steaks, about ¾ pound [350g] each

salt and freshly ground pepper

6 tablespoons plus 2 teaspoons peanut, vegetable or corn oil

1 or 2 yellow squash, about ½ pound [225g]

1 or 2 zucchini [*courgettes*], about ½ pound [225g]

1 sweet red or green pepper, cored and deseeded

3 ears fresh corn on the cob, or 1 cup [100g/4oz] cooked corn kernels

1 tablespoon imported mustard such as Dijon or Düsseldorf

2 tablespoons raspberry or red wine vinegar

1 tablespoon chopped fresh tarragon

1 cup [175g/6oz] thinly sliced onion rings

1½ cups [65g/2½oz] shredded Boston lettuce or, preferably, arugula [*rocket*]

Preheat a charcoal grill.

Sprinkle the steaks with salt and pepper to taste. Brush on all sides with 2 teaspoons of oil and set aside.

Trim the yellow squash and zucchini. Cut each squash and zucchini into 1½ inch [4cm] lengths. Cut each piece crosswise into ½ inch [1cm] slices. Stack the slices and cut them into ½ inch [1cm] 'sticks'. Set aside.

Cut the sweet pepper lengthwise into thin strips. Set aside.

Bring enough water to the boil to cover the squash, zucchini and sweet pepper when added. Add the vegetables. When the water returns to the boil, drain quickly. Run the vegetables under cold running water to chill briefly. Drain well.

Drop the ears of corn into boiling water. When the water returns to the boil, let simmer about 30 seconds. Drain. Cut the corn from the cob. Set aside.

Put the steaks on the grill, about 3 inches [7.5cm] from the source of heat. Broil [*grill*] about 3 to 4 minutes on one side. Turn and broil about 2 to 3 minutes on the other side. Remove the steaks from the grill. Trim off the fat from the steaks. Cut the steak on the diagonal (across the grain of the meat) into very thin slices. Set aside. Reserve any steak juices that flow from the meat.

Put the mustard in a mixing bowl and add the vinegar, stirring with a wire whisk. Beat in the remaining oil gradually. Add salt and pepper to taste and the tarragon.

Add the onion rings, corn, squash, zucchini, red or green pepper, steak and any steak juices. Stir to blend. Add a generous grinding of black pepper. Spoon the salad on to the centre of a serving dish. Garnish with shredded lettuce arranged around the salad. Serve at room temperature.

Camellia Panjabi

Palak Gosht

Lamb with Spinach

(50 Great Curries of India)

Indian food is so ubiquitous throughout the United Kingdom that some Indian dishes – chicken tikka is the best example – can probably now be considered British food. But while the flourishing of the neighbourhood curry restaurant has popularized Indian food, some of them peddle crude travesties of a great and varied school of cooking. Camellia Panjabi has been involved in two of London's most glamorous Indian restaurants – the Bombay Brasserie and Chutney Mary – and has helped Britain to rethink its ideas about 'high-class' Indian cooking.

You can consider this dish as a typical medium curry, neither too hot nor too complicated for moderately adventurous cooks and eaters.

What I find most interesting about the recipe is that the character of a curry comes not just from the quantity and types of spices that the cook uses but from the way in which they are used. As Camellia explains, the sequence in which you add the spices to the dish is critical 'because each spice has its own pattern of releasing flavour with heat ... If all the spices are added simultaneously, either some will burn or some will remain uncooked, meaning that the flavour remains unreleased.' This curry, which Camellia describes as 'earthy' and 'homestyle', has a really tremendous depth of flavour. She advises serving it with Indian bread rather than rice and I think it fits in perfectly well to a dinner with a Western first course and pudding.

Serves 4

675g/1¹/₂lb lamb

2cm x 5mm/ ³/₄ x ¹/₄ inch piece of fresh ginger

2 plump garlic cloves

1–2 green chillies

¹/₂ cup yoghurt

¹/₄ teaspoon cumin powder

200g/7oz spinach leaves or frozen puréed
    spinach

¹/₄ cup oil

1 cinnamon or bay leaf

1 black cardamom

2 cloves

225g/8oz onions, chopped

1 teaspoon coriander powder

¹/₂ teaspoon cumin powder

2 medium tomatoes, chopped

1 tablespoon tomato paste

1 teaspoon salt

a little nutmeg powder, to sprinkle

a knob of butter (optional)

Soak the lamb in warm water for 15 minutes to lighten the colour.

Purée the ginger, garlic and green chilli in a blender. Whisk the yoghurt and add to the ginger/garlic purée, together with the ¹/₄ teaspoon cumin powder.

Marinate the lamb in this mixture for at least 1 hour, longer if possible. Meanwhile, blanch the spinach in boiling water with a little salt for 10 seconds, drain and purée the spinach.

Heat the oil in a cooking pot with the cinnamon or bay leaf, cardamom and cloves. When the oil is really hot and the cinnamon leaf begins to fry, add the onions. Fry for 15 minutes over a low to moderate heat.

Add the coriander powder and sauté for 2 minutes, stirring continuously. Add the ¹/₂ teaspoon cumin powder and after 10 seconds add a little water. Allow the spices to cook.

Add the meat and its marinade, stir well and cook over a moderate heat for 10 minutes, until the yoghurt is absorbed. Sauté the meat for 3 minutes, stirring continuously, then add the tomatoes and tomato paste and cook for a couple of minutes. Add 1¹/₄ cups hot water and ³/₄ teaspoon of the salt. Turn the heat to low, cover with a lid and leave to simmer. When the meat is almost done, add the puréed spinach, taste for salt and mix well. Cook for 5 minutes, uncovered. When ready to serve, sprinkle with a little nutmeg powder and add a knob of butter if liked.

Irene Kuo

Scallion 'Exploded' Lamb

(The Key to Chinese Cooking)

Irene Kuo's *The Key to Chinese Cooking* is the greatest Chinese cookbook I have ever come across – a joy to read and a pleasure to use. Her scholarship, pragmatism and patient exposition of the intricacies of Chinese cooking put her in the pantheon of scholar-cooks alongside Julia Child, Anna del Conte and Claudia Roden. I also admire her lively style: 'shower in the scallions', she instructs, or 'quickly splash' or 'stir vigorously'. She is ideally equipped to be the poet laureate of a style of cooking that begins with an almost meditative preparation and climaxes in a frenzy of action. This recipe is a relief from the excellent but rather monotonous day-to-day lamb dishes that we cook most of the time. In her introduction Irene Kuo tells us that 'because of the marinating and the short cooking time, the lamb is very tender and full of flavour', and goes on to describe the dish as 'a wonderful robust northern speciality'. If you serve this as a main course you may need to double the quantities, as the recipe is intended to be one of many dishes in a typical Chinese dinner.

Serves 2–3

1 pound [450g] boneless leg of lamb or loin, trimmed of fat

1/2 pound [225g] whole medium scallions [*spring onions*]

4 large cloves garlic

5 tablespoons oil

For the marinade:

1/2 teaspoon salt

1 teaspoon roasted and crushed Szechuan peppercorns

2 tablespoons dark soy sauce

11/2 tablespoons dry sherry

For the seasoning sauce:

1 teaspoon sugar

1 tablespoon dark soy sauce

1 tablespoon dry sherry

1 tablespoon cider vinegar

1 tablespoon sesame oil

Cut the lamb across the grain into paper-thin slices about 2 inches [5cm] long and 1½ inches [4cm] wide. Place them in a deep bowl. Mix the marinade and pour it over the meat, stir to coat well, and let the lamb marinate for at least 30 minutes.

Trim off the root ends and then rinse and dry the scallions. Flatten the bulbs slightly with the side of a heavy knife, slit the white part in two lengthwise, and then cut the entire scallions crosswise into 1½ inch [4cm] long sections. Smash and peel the garlic. Mix the seasoning sauce in a bowl until the sugar is dissolved. Put all the ingredients on a working platter.

All the cutting preparations may be done in advance, but the seasoning sauce should not be mixed until you are ready to cook, lest the aroma of the vinegar dissipate. Any ingredients refrigerated should be brought to room temperature before stir-frying.

Stir-frying: heat a wok or large, heavy skillet [*frying pan*] over high heat until hot, about 30 seconds; add the oil, swirl and heat until hot. Lower the heat, add the garlic, and quickly stir and press the cloves in the hot oil for about 5 seconds. Turn up the heat again, scatter in the marinated meat, and stir and toss briskly for 10 seconds. Shower in the scallions; stir rapidly in tossing motions until their colour deepens and each piece is gleaming with oil. Then quickly splash in the seasoning sauce and stir vigorously for about 1 minute in sweeping and flipping motions until the meat and vegetables have absorbed most of the seasonings.

Pour the meat and scallions into a hot serving dish and serve immediately.

Frances Bissell
Leg of Lamb Andalusian Style
(The Real Meat Cookbook)

Frances Bissell began her cookery career as a devoted amateur and then, after winning the *Observer*/Mouton Cadet competition, came to prominence as *The Times* cook, following in the footsteps of the illustrious Katie Stewart. This recipe makes an exciting alternative to traditional roast leg of lamb for Sunday lunch and will certainly keep the oven cleaner. Frances suggests cooking it in a chicken brick, which you may now have to find at a car boot sale as many of these very useful relics of the Seventies have been rather sadly turfed out of our kitchens. The easiest way to remove the lemon zest is with a swivel vegetable peeler. To roast the peppers, core and quarter them, then shove them under a hot grill, skin-side up, until they blister and blacken. Put them under a tea towel to cool and the skin will slip off easily. Do let the joint rest before you carve: it's amazing what a little time spent waiting will do to the flavour of food.

Serves 6

2 onions, peeled and sliced
1 leg of lamb, weighing 1.75kg/4lb
1/2 lemon
salt
pepper
4 cloves of garlic, peeled and sliced
85ml/3fl oz olive oil

150ml/1/4 pint Manzanilla 'sherry'
1 red or green pepper, roasted, deseeded and sliced
3 ripe tomatoes, peeled, deseeded and chopped
1 bunch of fresh parsley (about 25g/1oz)
300ml/1/2 pint beer

Lay half the onion slices on the bottom of the cooking pot. Place the leg of lamb on top of them. Remove the zest of the lemon in strips and place them in the pot too. Rub the lamb all over with the lemon juice and season lightly with salt and pepper. Cut the garlic into slivers and insert these under the skin of the lamb and around the bone. Brush the lamb with the olive oil and pour on the Manzanilla. Cover carefully and marinate in the refrigerator overnight.

Next day, uncover the meat and let it come back to room temperature. Preheat the oven to 170–180°C/325–350°F/Gas Mark 3–4. Tuck the pepper and tomato around it. Reserve some of the parsley for decoration, but push the rest of it well down around the meat. Pour on the beer, put in the middle of the oven and cook for 30–35 minutes per 450g/1lb. Allow to rest before carving.

Towards the end of the cooking, you can cover the lamb with the lid or with a sheet of foil, if you like a moist joint, or leave the meat uncovered if you want it browned.

Vatcharin Bhumichitr

Pla Moo
Hot and Sour Pork Salad

(Vatch's Thai Cookbook)

An interesting counterpoint to our current fascination with Southeast-Asian cooking is the visit of the Thai king, Rama V, to Europe in 1897. As the first Asian monarch to visit Europe, Rama V was wined and dined in extravagant *fin de siècle* style by his brother royals. He returned to Thailand determined that his people should appreciate that great European staple, the potato, and he himself became particularly fond of tuna sandwiches. Today the culinary traffic flows in the opposite direction, and Southeast Asia provides us with a wealth of inspiring and stimulating tastes.

Thai cuisine features a number of warm salads, including this hot and sour pork salad, which you could also make with chicken. It is flavoured with *nam prik pow*, a powerful chilli oil used to spice up a number of Thai dishes, much as we might add a couple of drops of Tabasco or Worcestershire sauce to a stew. *Nam prik pow* is also delicious trickled on to a grilled steak or chicken breast and will keep well in the fridge. The small round aubergines the recipe calls for are completely different from the big, glossy, nearly black monsters that we import from Holland. Fortunately there are a growing number of Thai shops that can supply you with them: otherwise just leave them out of the recipe.

Serves 4

225g/8oz boneless pork, roughly chopped
2 tablespoons chicken stock
1 tablespoon *nam prik pow* (see below)
1 stalk of lemongrass, trimmed of all tough
   leaves, finely sliced into rings
4 small round green aubergines sliced into
   rounds
2 shallots, finely sliced
3 kaffir lime leaves, finely chopped

2 small fresh red or green chillies, finely
   chopped
1 tablespoon fish sauce
2 tablespoons lemon juice
1 tablespoon sugar
For the marinade:
2 garlic cloves, finely chopped
1 tablespoon oyster sauce
1 tablespoon fish sauce
1 tablespoon light soy sauce

Put all the marinade ingredients in a large bowl and stir well. Add the pork and leave to marinate for at least 1 hour.

Preheat the grill. Arrange the marinated pork on a rack set over a pan to catch the juices and grill until cooked, turning as necessary.

In a saucepan, heat the stock to boiling. Stir in the *nam prik pow* and add the pork with any juices. Stir in the remaining ingredients, mixing well. Turn on to a serving dish.

Nam Prik Pow
Grilled Chilli Oil

4 tablespoons vegetable oil
4 tablespoons finely chopped garlic
4 tablespoons finely chopped shallots
4 tablespoons finely chopped large dried red
   chillies

2 tablespoons dried shrimps
1 teaspoon salt
1 tablespoon sugar

In a wok or frying pan, heat the oil and fry the garlic until golden brown. Remove the garlic with a fine sieve and set aside. Add the shallots to the oil and fry until brown and crispy; remove with the sieve and set aside. Add the chillies to the oil and fry until they begin to darken; remove with the sieve.

In a mortar, pound the dried shrimps, then add the chillies, garlic and shallots and pound until thoroughly blended. Add this to the oil and stir over a low heat. Add the salt and stir to mix. Add the sugar and mix to make a thick, slightly oily, red/black sauce, not a paste.

Frances Bissell

Estouffade of Goat

(The Real Meat Cookbook)

You needn't really use goat – lamb is perfectly okay in this recipe. But given its delicious, gamey flavour I am astonished how many people are reluctant to eat goat. Maybe its gastronomic bad name has something to do with cartoon images of goats licking tin cans in rubbish dumps, or perhaps the historic demonology of the devil/goat remains with us. If you are able to find goat – look for a butcher near a biggish West Indian community – do try it. Kid will be tender but a little less flavourful.

An estouffade is a worthy, old-fashioned French way of cooking meat slowly in a tiny amount of liquid. In this recipe you marinate the meat overnight and then the cooking consists of little more than a few minutes' worth of effort and a bit of pot watching. The cooking time in the oven should be about 1½ hours. Frances Bissell recommends serving noodles with the dish. I would also propose orzo, that lovely rice-shaped Greek pasta, or some garlic mashed potatoes.

Serves 4

450g/1lb leg or shoulder of goat, off the bone
12 stoned black olives
a few button onions or 1 onion, peeled and
   sliced (optional)
seasoning
For the marinade:
1 onion
1 carrot

1 celery stalk
4 cloves of garlic (or more, to taste)
300ml/½ pint dry white wine
85ml/3fl oz extra virgin olive oil
1 sprig of rosemary or lavender
1 bay leaf
thyme or oregano

Peel and chop the vegetables for the marinade and put them in a saucepan with the wine and olive oil. Bring to the boil and simmer for 2–3 minutes. Remove from the heat and allow to cool down. Meanwhile dice the meat and put it in a bowl with the herbs. Pour over it the cooled marinade, cover and refrigerate overnight.

Drain the meat from the marinade. Wipe it dry and fry it all over in a flameproof casserole to brown it. Add the olives and a few small onions (or sliced onion) if you like, and strain the marinade over it.

Simmer or cook in a low oven until the meat is tender. Season and serve with fresh broad pasta such as pappardelle or tagliatelle.

Margaret Costa

The Epicure's Kidneys

(Margaret Costa's Four Seasons Cookery Book)

By an immense stroke of luck, the first day I arrived in London to begin my postgraduate studies I was taken to lunch in a little basement restaurant called Lacy's. I knew from assiduous study of Humphrey Lyttleton's restaurant column in *Queen* magazine (one of the ancestors of today's *Harpers & Queen*) that Lacy's was one of a handful of trendsetting restaurants in London. It was a husband-and-wife operation, run by food writer Margaret Costa (front of house) and Bill Lacy (in the kitchen). I met Margaret that day and became a regular customer. Bill was a very talented chef but Margaret was the creative powerhouse of the establishment. Her major work, *The Four Seasons Cookery Book*, only recently came back into print and Margaret was

inexplicably and unjustly overlooked for many years. She is one of the greatest cookery writers of our time and her book is full of delicious, forthright recipes clearly and confidently explained.

I have sometimes eaten kidneys for breakfast in cold country houses but I would hardly count myself a great fan of them. However, this recipe of Margaret's is nicely old-fashioned and almost tailormade for adventurous budget cooking. I am also amused by the pre-politically correct way in which Margaret writes: 'Kidneys have always seemed to me a very masculine kind of food, perhaps because their flavour is so strong and pronounced.'

8 lamb's kidneys	salt and black pepper
butter	1 tablespoon Dijon mustard
1 small shallot	1 dessertspoon redcurrant jelly
20g/³/₄oz flour	2 tablespoons thick cream
150ml/¹/₄ pint good stock	1 tablespoon port

Slice the kidneys; put them in a basin and cover them with boiling water. Leave for 2 minutes. Drain, dry, skin and core. Cut them into slices or fairly large dice. Melt 30g/a good ounce of butter and cook the kidneys in it for a few minutes until they are lightly coloured all over.

Remove them from the pan, add the chopped shallot and cook for a few minutes until it softens; blend in the flour and gradually add the stock. Simmer to make a smooth and creamy sauce. Season well. Stir in the mustard, the redcurrant jelly, the cream and the port. (Failing port, use a medium-dry sherry or Madeira.) Reheat the kidneys very gently in the sauce; it must on no account be allowed to boil or the kidneys will toughen. Serve on a big bed of fluffy boiled rice into which you have stirred some freshly grated nutmeg and a little butter, just allowed to turn nut-brown in another pan. Mushrooms are the ideal accompaniment to this dish.

Involtini con Funghi
Veal Rolls with Wild Mushrooms

(A Passion for Mushrooms)

Through a series of television programmes Antonio Carluccio has become the most familiar propagandist for Italian cooking in Britain. But before such celebrity he was better known as a mushroom-mad restaurateur, delicatessen owner, and brother-in-law of Terence Conran. Without a doubt he has done more than anyone to wake Britain up to the fact that wild mushrooms are not just for scavenging European peasants. Keen mushroom hunters now fill — some might say overfill — British woodlands and Antonio finds chanterelles and porcini on motorway verges. The rest of us have to buy the wretched things, and find them expensive and a pain in the neck to clean, but extremely delicious.

This recipe comes from *A Passion for Mushrooms*, which is a first-rate reference book as well as being stuffed with good recipes. I like this splendidly old-fashioned dish. Make sure that your butcher cuts the veal escalopes from a complete muscle so that they stay together when beaten flat. If you do the beating yourself (and this applies to chicken as well as veal) put the escalopes between two sheets of greaseproof paper to protect the meat and prevent it tearing. Clingfilm works too, but foil often splits after a hard bash from a rolling pin. Veal tends to dry out when it is cooked so this recipe includes Mortadella to keep it moist. After you take the cooked veal rolls and mushrooms out of the pan you could deglaze it by stirring in a little dry vermouth or white wine, bringing it to the boil, then adding a couple of tablespoons of mascarpone to make a little sauce.

Serves 4

8 thin slices of veal (weighing about 450g/1lb), beaten flat enough to roll around the filling ingredients, plus some wooden cocktail sticks to secure them

For the filling:

1 tablespoon finely chopped parsley

2 thickly cut slices Mortadella, cut into very small cubes

2 cornichons, very finely chopped

10 capers, very finely chopped

salt and pepper to taste

For the mushrooms:

4 tablespoons olive oil

1 small onion, finely chopped

1 clove garlic, finely chopped

225g/8oz very small, cleaned, wild mushrooms

1 tablespoon chopped parsley

Take care that the slices of veal to be rolled are beaten out flat between sheets of plastic on a work surface and do not show any holes. Thoroughly mix the filling ingredients and spread some evenly on each slice. Roll the veal carefully and hold firmly in place with a cocktail stick. Fry the rolls in the olive oil until brown on each side and set aside. In the same pan, fry the onion first, adding the garlic when the onion is almost cooked, and then the mushrooms; stir-fry over low heat for 5–6 minutes, add the meat rolls and tablespoonful of parsley and serve hot.

Honey-roasted Pork

(Cuisine des Quatre Saisons)

Along with Alain Ducasse, who has described him as 'the Flaubert of the kitchens', Joel Robuchon is at the pinnacle of modern French cooking. Like Ducasse – and indeed that other betoqued titan, Paul Bocuse – he has enthusiastically used traditional home cooking as the basis of his own high-flying cuisine. Despite the enormous success of his Parisian restaurant – three Michelin rosettes and a daunting waiting list for would-be patrons – Robuchon astonished the gastronomic world by retiring to concentrate on cookery writing. (He sold his restaurant, by the way, to Alain Ducasse.) His *Cuisine des Quatre Saisons* is as fine a chef-written cookbook as you can buy, full of authority and ingenuity.

Like many exponents of *cuisine de terroir* (cooking that reflects and respects local products and traditions), Robuchon has helped the pig make a comeback in upmarket kitchens: his pig's head was one of the late President Mitterrand's favourite dishes and indeed Mitterrand awarded him the Légion d'honneur. For decades pork was not seen on the best menus in France; now it is ubiquitous. This simple-sounding roast is a textbook example of the most basic cooking – roasting a joint – raised to the highest possible level. Turning convention upside down, Robuchon salts the joint first to intensify its flavour. He then roasts it at two different temperatures, moderately hot to start and then much hotter for the glazing. As with other roasts, it is vital that you let it rest before you carve it.

'Fresh pork,' Robuchon writes, 'should be served well done: juicy, but white without a trace of pink. Served hot, it is delicious, but pork is perhaps even better cold as long as it cools in the open air under a protective sheet of aluminium foil rather than in the refrigerator.' Robuchon has over 100 potato recipes in his repertoire. I'd serve this with mash.

Serves 6

3lb/1.5kg loin of pork, with broken bones
3 cloves garlic, cut into slivers
12 sage leaves
salt and pepper
2 sprigs thyme
2 tablespoons groundnut oil

2 medium-sized onions
1 bouquet garni
1 large carrot, sliced crosswise
2 tablespoons honey
2 spoonfuls red wine vinegar

Prepare the pork the night before. Insert slivers of garlic all over the joint. Roll the sage leaves between your palms and then season them with salt and pepper. With the point of a small knife, make small slits between the ribs and insert the sage leaves.

Rub the roast with salt and thyme. Wrap it in clingfilm and place it in the refrigerator. The salt will have the effect of ageing the meat and bringing out the flavours of the herbs and garlic.

The next day, take the roast out of the refrigerator, wipe it and let it come back to room temperature.

Heat the oil in a casserole over a medium heat. When it is hot, place the loin of pork and the broken bones in the casserole. Let the meat brown, turning it from time to time. Add the onions and the bouquet garni. Cook for 3 or 4 minutes.

Cover the casserole and put it in the oven, which has been preheated to 200°C/400°F/Gas Mark 6. Let it roast for 1½ hours, turning it often. Take the meat out and season with pepper. Deglaze the pot with 300ml/½ pint of water and let it boil lightly for 12 to 15 minutes until it has reduced by half.

Place the roast on the oven door. Turn the thermostat up to 240°C/475°F/Gas Mark 9. Dissolve the honey with the vinegar and baste the roast. Put it back in the oven for 12 to 16 minutes, basting it often. Let the meat sit for 15 to 30 minutes before carving.

To serve, carve the roast and arrange the slices on a warm serving dish. Pass the juice through a sieve and serve it in a gravy boat.

Irene Kuo

Chicken Fu Yung Sauce for Vegetables

(The Key to Chinese Cooking)

As you can tell from the name of this recipe, it is hardly vegetarian, but it is an intriguing dish to serve up to meat eaters who find themselves turning towards more vegetables. One chicken breast makes enough sauce for four helpings of vegetables. Irene Kuo explains that 'this is a sauce version of that northern specialty Fu Yung Chicken … this creamy sauce lends elegance to many vegetables such as peas, lima beans, cauliflower, broccoli and asparagus'. Add it to any vegetable stir-fry, briefly stir-frying the sauce with the vegetables just before serving. Ingredients and preparation are straightforward but you will need to know that 'march-chopping' requires a heavy knife or Chinese cleaver and means that you should chop up and down firmly from one side of the chicken breast to the other.

Serves 4

¼ pound [*100g*] boneless and skinless chicken breast
¼ teaspoon salt
1 teaspoon dry sherry

2 teaspoons cornstarch [*cornflour*] dissolved in 2 teaspoons water
4 egg whites, beaten until light and frothy

Place the chicken breast, smooth-side down, on a chopping board and scrape it with a sharp knife or spoon in light strokes; discard tendon and any membrane. Pile the shaved meat and cut it closely; then sprinkle a teaspoon of water over it and march-chop with a wet knife or cleaver until the consistency is pasty.

Put the meat in a large, deep bowl; add the salt, sherry and dissolved cornstarch and mix until smooth. Then add the beaten egg whites little by little, stirring vigorously until the mixture is completely smooth. Let the mixture marinate in the refrigerator for 30 minutes or longer – this can be done hours ahead of time. Before you add it to any vegetable bring it to room temperature and stir vigorously to fluff it up.

Julia Child, Simone Beck and Louisette Bertholle

Poulet Sauté
Sautéed Chicken

(Mastering the Art of French Cooking)

This is the first recipe I ever cooked and I had three good reasons for trying it: I liked poulet sauté; at the time I wanted to be an academic and the length and exactness of the recipe were reassuring; and finally Julia Child was one of my television idols. Gangly, authoritative and with an accent that made me sound pedestrian, Julia was the colossus who bestrode the American television kitchen for years with a series of hit programmes beginning with 'The French Chef'. But before television celebrity she ran a cooking school with her chums Bertholle and Beck, and together they produced the monumental two-volume *Mastering the Art of French Cooking* – one of the small handful of books that no cook should be without. The first time I cooked this recipe it worked perfectly and it has continued to work perfectly for me for 20 years. It may be long but it is an absolute model of clarity. In this cookbook, and in all her subsequent ones written without Beck and Bertholle, Julia Child has been the best possible mentor for nervous and experienced cooks alike – always with you in the kitchen, as it were, reassuring, cajoling, educating, strict but gentle. She is the greatest.

Serves 4–6
Total cooking time: 30 to 35 minutes.

Browning the chicken (8 to 10 minutes)
1.25–1.5kg/2¹/₂–3lb cut-up frying chicken
Dry each piece of chicken thoroughly. It will
   not brown if it is damp.
a heavy 25cm/10 inch casserole, frying pan, or
   electric frying pan

25g/1oz butter and 1 dessertspoon oil, more if
   necessary to keep bottom of pan filmed
   with fat
tongs for turning the chicken

Place the casserole or frying pan over moderately high heat with the butter and oil (360°F/185°C for an electric frying pan). When you see that the butter foam has almost subsided, add as many chicken pieces, skin-side down, as will fit easily in one layer. In 2 to 3 minutes, when the chicken has browned to a nice golden colour on one side, turn it to brown on another side. Regulate heat so that fat is always very hot but not burning. Remove browned pieces as they are done and add fresh ones until all pieces have browned.

Finishing the cooking (20 to 25 minutes)
salt and pepper
optional: 1–2 teaspoons fresh green herbs:
   thyme, basil, and tarragon, or tarragon

only; or 1 teaspoon dried herbs
25–40g/1–1¹/₂oz butter, if necessary

Season the dark meat with salt, pepper, and optional herbs. (The wings and breasts are done later, as they cook faster.) If the browning fat has burned, pour it out of the casserole and add the fresh butter. Place over moderate heat (300°F/150°C for an electric frying pan). Add the dark meats, cover the casserole, and cook slowly for 8 to 9 minutes.

salt and pepper
a bulb baster

Season the white meat, add it to the dark meat, and baste the chicken with the butter in the casserole. Cover and continue cooking for about 15 minutes, turning and basting the chicken 2 or 3 times.

   The meat is done when the fattest part of the drumsticks is tender if pinched and the chicken juices run clear yellow when the meat is pricked deeply with a fork.

   Remove the chicken to a hot serving dish. Cover and keep warm for 2 to 3 minutes while finishing the sauce.

Brown deglazing sauce

1 tablespoon chopped shallots or spring
    onions
optional: 150ml/¹/₄ pint dry white wine or
    65ml/¹/₈ pint dry white vermouth

150–300ml/¹/₄–¹/₂ pint brown chicken stock,
    beef bouillon, or tinned chicken broth
15–25g/¹/₂–1oz softened butter
optional: 1–2 tablespoons chopped parsley or
    fresh green herbs

Remove all but about 2 tablespoons of fat from the casserole. Add the shallots or spring onions and cook slowly for 1 minute. Pour in the optional wine, and the stock. Raise heat and boil rapidly, scraping up coagulated sauté juices and reducing liquid to about 65ml/¹/₈ pint. Correct seasoning. Remove from heat and just before serving, swirl in the enrichment butter and optional herbs.

Arrange around the dish whatever vegetables you have chosen. Pour the sauce over the chicken and serve.

For a wait of up to half an hour
Finish the sauce except for its final buttering. Arrange the cooked chicken in an enamelled, glazed, ovenglass or stainless steel casserole and baste it with the sauce. Cover loosely and place over barely simmering water. Just before serving, and away from heat, tip casserole, add enrichment butter, and baste the chicken with the sauce.

Partial cooking in advance
The chicken may be browned, the dark meat cooked for 8 to 9 minutes, and the white meat added and cooked for 5 minutes more. Then leave the casserole aside, uncovered. About 10 to 15 minutes before serving time, cover and finish the cooking on top of the stove; or heat the casserole and set it in a preheated 180°C/350°F/Gas Mark 4 oven for 15–20 minutes.

Claire Macdonald

Stir-fried Chicken with Ginger, Cardamom and Cashew Nuts

(Suppers)

Claire Macdonald is a wonderful cook, with her head in the clouds of the global larder and her feet firmly planted on the Isle of Skye, where she and her husband Godfrey (who is the Chief of the Name and Arms of Macdonald, the largest of the highland clans) run the most charming hotel in Scotland. Although she is a passionate advocate of Scottish produce and cooking, a lot of Claire's food is what I would call sensibly cosmopolitan. This dish may have hints of Thai, Chinese and Indian cookery but it doesn't require any particularly exotic techniques or equipment: she has a real knack for keeping on the home-cooking side of the restaurant food threshold. I'm a great fan of her chatty, enthusiastic writing style. You can't help smiling at the autobiographical note in this list of ingredients when she specifies '8 chicken breasts (for growing offspring, 1 chicken breast per person isn't quite enough)'.

Serves 6

8 chicken breasts (for growing offspring, 1 chicken breast per person isn't quite enough), each breast sliced into as thin matchsticks as possible

about 18 spring onions, each trimmed and sliced into thin sticks

4 cardamom seeds, crushed (with the end of a rolling pin or in a pestle and mortar)

5cm/2 inch fresh root ginger, pared of its skin and finely chopped

1–2 cloves of garlic (depending on your taste), peeled and finely chopped

3 teaspoons cornflour

3 tablespoons strong soy sauce

2 tablespoons dry sherry

300ml/½ pint chicken stock

3 tablespoons sunflower oil

75g/3oz cashew nuts, chopped and fried in butter and salt till golden brown – or bought already salted, then chopped

Put the strips of chicken, sliced spring onions, crushed cardamom, chopped ginger and garlic in a bowl, and mix together well. Mix together the cornflour, soy sauce, sherry and stock. Leave for several hours.

Heat the oil in a large, deep frying or sauté pan, add the chicken, spring onions, ginger and garlic mixture, and stir-fry in the very hot oil till the strips of chicken turn opaque. Then pour in the cornflour and liquids – stirring this mixture up well before you add it because the cornflour tends to sink to the bottom. Stir till the sauce boils, then dish up the contents of the pan (or wok) into a warmed serving dish and scatter the chopped cashew nuts over the surface.

Serve with boiled basmati rice, and a salad – a green salad containing chopped oranges and snipped chives seems to go very well with this stir-fry.

Paula Wolfert

Chicken Kdra with Almonds and Chickpeas

(Couscous and Other Good Food from Morocco)

For some time now the more daring food futurists have been betting heavily on Moroccan cooking as the next trend, predicting that the complexity, sophistication and originality of this cuisine would find a worldwide audience. So far there have been glimmers of North Africa in some of London and New York's hipper restaurants but Moroccan food has yet to hit the big time. The American food writer Paula Wolfert is the evangelist for Morocco in the English-speaking world. Like Claudia Roden she is a scholar-cook. She explains in her book *Good Food from Morocco* that 'a *kdra* is a certain type of tagine, cooked with the strong Moroccan butter called *smen*, a lot of onions reduced to butter softness, spiced with pepper and saffron, and usually "cut" at the end with a dash of lemon juice. The stews of many couscous dishes are based on the principles of the *kdra* sauce, as are some of the most famous dishes in the Moroccan repertoire.'

A word about equipment and ingredients. A tagine, the traditional cooking vessel for this dish, is an earthenware pot with a tall conical top like a dunce's cap. Steam rising from the simmering dish condenses in the top and falls back on to the food, keeping it moist. Neat. Buy one if you like collecting kit – I do – otherwise use any covered crock. *Smen* is rather like the Indian *ghee*. Not just clarified butter, but butter oil without milk solids that has been heated to concentrate its flavour. The idea of mixing saffron with some turmeric is a good one. The turmeric enhances the colour and perhaps originally was used to reduce the prohibitive cost of saffron as a flavouring. To pulverize saffron, heat it in a dry frying pan for about 30 seconds and then crush it with your fingers.

I confess to not being totally crazy about cooked almonds in savoury dishes, so I leave them out of this recipe. (I would make a lousy Moroccan: Paula Wolfert cites another version of this dish with no chickpeas and *twice* as many almonds.) As with all stews you can cook this ahead and leave it in the fridge. I'd serve it with couscous or rice.

Serves 4–5

165g/5¹/₂oz blanched whole almonds

165g/5¹/₂oz dried chickpeas, soaked
  overnight, or 275g/10oz tin cooked
  chickpeas

¹/₄ teaspoon pulverized saffron (mixed with a
  little turmeric)

salt to taste

1 teaspoon white pepper

¹/₂ teaspoon powdered ginger

1 large cinnamon stick

3 tablespoons butter or 2 tablespoons *smen*

1 chicken (1.5–1.6kg/3–3¹/₂lb), quartered, or
  2 sets of chicken legs and thighs, or
  3 squabs, or 6 Moroccan pigeons

2 Spanish onions, quartered lengthwise and
  finely sliced

900ml/1¹/₂ pints chicken stock or water, more
  if necessary

4 tablespoons chopped parsley

juice of 1 lemon, or to taste

Cover the almonds with cold water and simmer, covered, for at least 2 hours. (The cooking time is approximate – it depends upon the freshness of the almonds.)

In a separate saucepan, cover the soaked and drained chickpeas with fresh cold water, bring to boil, reduce the heat, and simmer, covered, 1 hour. Drain and submerge in a bowl of cold water. Rub the chickpeas to remove their skins. The skins will rise to the surface. Discard them. (If you are using tinned chickpeas, rinse, drain and skin them, and set them aside.)

In a large casserole combine half the saffron, salt, the spices, butter or *smen*, and the prepared poultry. Cook over low heat, without browning, for 2 to 3 minutes. Chop 4 or 5 slices of onion finely and add to the casserole with the stock. Bring to the boil, add the drained, skinned chickpeas, and simmer for 30 minutes, covered. (Do not add the tinned chickpeas until the poultry has finished cooking.)

Add the remaining sliced onions and chopped parsley and continue cooking 30 minutes more, or until the poultry is very tender (the flesh almost falling off the bone). Transfer the poultry to a warm serving dish. Add the tinned chickpeas to the sauce. By boiling rapidly, reduce the sauce in the casserole to a thick gravy.

Drain the almonds and add to the sauce, along with remaining saffron. Cook together for 1 or 2 minutes and spoon over the poultry. Sprinkle with lemon juice to cut the richness of the sauce. Serve hot.

Marcella Hazan

Roast Chicken with Lemons

(The Essentials of Classic Italian Cooking)

In the late 20th century, chicken has become almost our universal protein. Few people other than committed vegetarians object to it, so the safest bet for feeding any number of people – from dinner-party guests to crowds at a wedding – has to be chicken. Consequently there are never enough chicken recipes. This is one of the all-time greats. As Marcella Hazan says, 'If this were a still-life its title could be "Chicken with Two Lemons". That is all there is in it. No fat to cook with, no basting to do, no stuffing to prepare, no condiments except for salt and pepper.' It is amazingly juicy and flavourful, but you must make it exactly accord-

ing to the recipe. When you roast a chicken upside down for the first half hour the juices running down over the breast baste it for you. Remember to let the chicken rest for a good 10 minutes before you serve it – this will firm up the flesh and make it easier to carve. Finally, this is the perfect opportunity to get the best genuine free-range chicken your butcher (or supermarket) can supply and you can afford. Like any roast chicken it is best served with a green salad, simply dressed. Eat the salad on the same plate as the chicken and the warm juices will mingle beautifully with your salad greens.

Serves 4

a 1.5–1.75kg/3–4lb chicken
salt
freshly ground black pepper

2 rather small lemons
trussing needle and string

Preheat the oven to 180°C/350°F/Gas Mark 4.

Wash the chicken thoroughly inside and out with cold water. Remove all the bits of fat hanging loose. Let the bird sit for about 10 minutes on a slightly tilted plate to drain all the water out of it. Thoroughly pat it dry all around with a tea towel or kitchen paper.

Sprinkle a generous amount of salt and black pepper on the chicken, rubbing it in with your fingers over all its body and into its cavity.

Wash the lemons in cold water and dry them with a tea towel. Soften each lemon by placing it on a counter and rolling it back and forth while at the same time putting firm downwards pressure on it with the palm of your hand. Puncture each of the lemons in at least 20 places, using a sturdy round cocktail stick, a trussing needle, a sharp-pointed fork or similar implement.

Place both lemons in the bird's cavity. Close up the opening with cocktail sticks or with a trussing needle and string. Close it well but don't make an absolutely airtight job of it because the air inside expands as it becomes hot and if it has nowhere to go it may cause the chicken to burst. Run kitchen string from one leg to the other, tying it at both knuckle ends. Leave the legs in their natural position without pulling them tight. If the

skin is unbroken, the chicken will puff up as it cooks, and the string serves only to keep the thighs from spreading apart and splitting the skin.

Put the chicken into a roasting pan, breast-side down. Do not add cooking fat of any kind. This bird is self-basting, so you need not fear it will stick to the pan. Place it in the upper third of the preheated oven. After 30 minutes, turn the chicken over to have the breast face up. When turning it, try not to puncture the skin. If kept intact, the chicken will swell like a balloon, which makes for an arresting presentation at the table later. Do not worry too much about it, however, because even if it fails to swell, the flavour will not be affected.

Cook for another 30–35 minutes, then turn the oven thermostat up to 200°C/400°F/ Gas Mark 6, and cook for an additional 20 minutes. Calculate between 20 and 25 minutes' total cooking time for each 450g/1lb. There is no need to turn the chicken again.

Whether your bird has puffed up or not, bring it to the table whole and leave the lemons inside until it is carved and opened. The juices that run out are perfectly delicious, so be sure to spoon them over the chicken slices. The lemons will have shrivelled up but they still contain some juice; do not squeeze them, they may squirt.

Martha Stewart

Roast Turkey with Mosaic of Sage

(The Martha Stewart Cookbook)

It is tempting to postulate an apostolic succession of women who taught America to cook, beginning with the deliciously named Victorian cook from Boston, Fanny Farmer. Martha Stewart would fit neatly into the pattern as the latest and perhaps the most successful of them all. But she is far more than just a cook, and I could without exaggeration call her a phenomenon of a culinary, social and commercial kind. She is in fact 'homemaker in chief' to the American people, a sort of überhousewife whose ideas about the good life have been propagated through cookbooks, her own glossy monthly magazine, television programmes and merchandise ranging from bedlinen to gardening tools. I once watched one of those confessional chat shows on American television, where a number of women admitted to feeling inadequate because they couldn't live up to Martha Stewart's standards. Needless to say, her success arouses a lot of envy and resentment, and there has even been a 'revisionist' biography of her which enjoyed some notoriety. Critics dismiss her as derivative and glib, or grudgingly concede that she is 'practical'. Humbug. Martha Stewart's success is based on nothing less than careful methodology, ceaseless anticipation of possible pitfalls, writing of extreme clarity, and an unerring sense of what tastes good. This recipe certainly tastes good and is one of the best and most interesting ways of roasting a turkey. If you don't like sage, use flat-leaf parsley, basil or lovage instead. Coarse kosher salt is American for sea salt.

Serves 12–14

one 18–20 pound [*8–9kg*] fresh turkey
1 tablespoon extra virgin olive oil
20 fresh sage leaves
coarse kosher salt

any stuffing
12 tablespoons [*175g/6oz*] unsalted butter,
  melted, for basting
2 cups [*500ml/17fl oz*] dry vermouth

Preheat the oven to 350°F [*180°C/Gas Mark 4*].

Remove the neck and gizzards from inside the turkey and rinse the bird thoroughly with cold water. Pat dry. Rub the olive oil over the entire surface of the turkey. Using your fingers, gently loosen the skin of the turkey from the breast and drumsticks. Carefully arrange individual layers of sage under the skin in a mosaic pattern. Lightly salt the cavity.

Turn the turkey breast-side down and loosely stuff the neck cavity with about 2 cups [*500ml/17fl oz*] of stuffing. Pull the neck skin over the cavity and fasten it to the back of the turkey with skewers or wooden picks. Turn the turkey breast-side up and fold the wing tips underneath the turkey so that the tips are almost touching. Lightly stuff the main cavity with stuffing. Place a double layer of aluminium foil over the exposed stuffing and tie the drumsticks together with kitchen string.

Place the turkey on a rack in a large roasting pan lined with aluminium foil and generously brush with melted butter. Roast the turkey, basting every 30 minutes with melted butter and pan juices, for about 5 hours, or until an instant-read thermometer inserted in the thigh registers 175–180°F [*79–82°C*]. During the last half hour, add the dry vermouth to the pan. If the turkey legs or breast brown too quickly, cover them lightly with foil.

Transfer the turkey to a cutting board, reserving the pan juices for gravy. Remove the stuffing, tent the turkey with foil, and allow it to sit for 20 to 30 minutes before carving.

Martin Webb and Richard Whittington
Shichimi-spiced Duck and Escarole Salad with Ginger Vinaigrette

(The Fusion)

Martin Webb, an excellent Australian-trained chef, teamed up with Richard Whittington (who has co-written with Alastair Little) on a book before going back Down Under.

Pan-frying is one of the most valuable cooking techniques. Get yourself a heavy ridged grill pan (it will help you make those nice criss-cross markings you get on grilled food in restaurants) or make do with any decent nonstick frying pan. Keep an eye on the heat and you can ring any number of changes with chunks of protein such as tuna steaks, chops and poultry breasts, using various marinades and quick pan sauces.

If possible, use the more flavourful Barbary duck breasts for this recipe – you can find them in good supermarkets – and, unless you are hugely hungry, one breast will feed two. Otherwise use the smaller Lincolnshire duck. When frying duck it is often a good idea to slash the skin in three or four places because it enables the marinade to seep into the flesh and also lets the fat drain away a bit more efficiently as the duck is cooked. Letting the duck rest for at least 10 minutes before cutting really helps the flavour and tenderness. Shichimi is a Japanese spice mix containing chilli and, typically, roasted sesame seeds, sansho pepper, dried orange rind and poppy seeds. It is available from Japanese food shops.

Serves 4

2 large duck breasts
1 tablespoon sunflower oil
2 teaspoons shichimi
1 head of escarole, separated
salt and pepper

For the ginger vinaigrette:

1 tablespoon rice vinegar
5cm/2 inch piece of ginger, sliced
4 tablespoons sunflower oil

Brush the duck breasts with oil, then rub the shichimi mix into both sides with ½ teaspoon of salt. Leave for 30 minutes at room temperature to absorb the flavours.

Over a low heat in a nonstick pan, place the duck breasts skin-side down and cook for 10 minutes without moving them. Turn and give them another 5 minutes. Turn again, increase the heat and crisp the skin for 2–3 minutes. Transfer to a cutting board, skin-side up, and leave for 10–15 minutes.

Put the escarole leaves into a large bowl. In a separate small bowl, make the dressing: dissolve ½ teaspoon salt and ¼ teaspoon ground pepper in the vinegar. In a food processor, blitz the ginger with the oil. Pass through a sieve into the bowl with the vinegar, working as much of the pulp through as you can with the back of a spoon. Whisk to amalgamate, pour over the escarole and toss to coat.

Turn the duck skin-side down and carve into thick slices at an angle. Mound the leaves on 4 plates and arrange the sliced duck on top.

Pierre Koffman

Canard aux Pêches
Roast Duck with Peaches

(Memories of Gascony)

The reticent and intellectual Pierre Koffman is one of the finest French chefs ever to work in Great Britain. His first cookbook, *Memories of Gascony*, is a great, elegiacal work – a sort of *À la Recherche du temps perdu* well lubricated with duck fat. While I sometimes find Gascon cuisine too overpowering a hymn to confit and terrine, Koffman's account of his childhood on the farm is a guaranteed appetite enhancer. 'There were about a hundred ducks on the farm,' he writes, 'and it was my job, after the harvest, to drive them out to feed in the stubble fields, and to make certain that none of them got lost. It was a difficult thing to do, because ducks are not as obedient as geese, and they rush all over the field in every direction, just as they please. I was armed with a long stick, with which I had to try to keep them together.' The young Koffman was proud never to have lost a duck and recalls how duck was an occasional treat, especially for Sunday lunch in the summertime.

This recipe for duck with peaches is simple and elegant, with the sugar and acidity of the fruit neatly balancing the richly flavoured duck. As with any simple recipe, the choice of ingredients is all. Buy the best duck you can – it needn't come from France, there are perfectly good British ducks on the market, especially Trelough and Gressingham – and make sure you get really good peaches as well. When making the sauce it's important to boil the vinegar until it has evaporated, then to boil the wine until it has thickened and become slightly syrupy.

Serves 4

1 duck, about 2–2.5kg/4¹/₂–5¹/₂lb
salt and freshly ground pepper
2 large peaches
300ml/¹/₂ pint dry white wine

50g/2oz sugar
2 tablespoons Armagnac
50ml/2fl oz wine vinegar

Preheat the oven to 230°C/450°F/Gas Mark 8. Season the duck inside and out and roast in the hot oven for about 55 minutes.

Peel, stone and halve the peaches. Heat the wine and sugar, put in the peaches and poach until tender. Set aside.

When the duck is cooked, transfer to a serving dish and pour the Armagnac into the cavity. Cover the duck with foil and keep warm.

Pour off the fat in the roasting pan, then pour in the vinegar and reduce completely, taking care that it does not burn. Add the wine in which you poached the peaches and reduce by half. Check the seasoning.

Slice the peaches and arrange them around the duck. Pour over the sauce and serve.

Rick Bayless

Codornices Asadas en Mole de Cacahuale
Smoky Peanut *Mole* with Grilled Quail

(Rick Bayless's Mexican Kitchen)

Rick Bayless is very much in the tradition of Julia Child, explaining the arcana of a school of cookery – in his case Mexican – with patience, exactitude and great attention to detail. When it comes to cooking, this sort of recipe writing is distance learning at its best.

A *mole* is a savoury, chilli-spiked Mexican sauce. Perhaps the most celebrated one is the delicious bitter chocolate *mole* which comes from the picture-postcard town of Oaxaca. This peanut *mole* may sound a bit weird but not if you think of it as an analogue to the peanut and chilli sauce that we eat with chicken satay.

Although the public face of Mexican cooking in Britain remains mired in the Margarita-soaking-up variety of tortilla, there must be an underground of keen Mexican cooks because you can now buy more interesting varieties of Mexican chillies than ever before. The chipotles in this recipe have an alluring smoky tang which goes especially well with peanuts. Rick Bayless recommends this as 'the easiest *mole* I know and its crowd-pleasing flavours go well with everything from chicken, quail and duck to pork, swordfish and grouper'.

Serves 6

2 medium (about 1 ounce [25g] total) dried ancho chillies, stemmed and deseeded
4 tablespoons vegetable or olive oil
½ small white onion, sliced
2 garlic cloves, peeled
8 ounces [225g] (about 1 medium-large round or 3–4 plum) ripe tomatoes
1 cup [100g/4oz] dry roasted peanuts, plus a few tablespoons chopped for garnish
2 slices firm white bread (or ½ dry Mexican bolillo roll), torn into pieces
2 canned chipotle chillies en adobo, deseeded
⅛ teaspoon allspice, preferably freshly ground
½ teaspoon cinnamon, preferably freshly ground Mexican canela
about 3½ cups [900ml/1½ pints] chicken broth
½ cup [120ml/4fl oz] fruity red wine
1 tablespoon cider vinegar
2 bay leaves
salt, about 1½ teaspoons, depending on the saltiness of the broth
sugar, about 1 tablespoon
12 partially boned, good-size quail (I like ones that are at least 4 ounces [100g] each)
a little freshly ground black pepper
sprigs of flat-leaf parsley, for garnish

The peanut *mole*: tear the ancho chillies into flat pieces, then toast a few at a time on an ungreased griddle or skillet [*frying pan*] over medium heat; press flat with a metal spatula for a few seconds, until they crackle and change colour slightly, then flip, and press again. (If they give off more than the slightest wisp of smoke, they are burning and will add a bitter element to the sauce.) In a small bowl, cover the chillies with hot water and let rehydrate for 30 minutes, stirring occasionally to ensure even soaking. Drain and discard the water.

Meanwhile heat 1 tablespoon of the oil in a heavy, medium-size pot over medium heat. Add the onion and garlic cloves and fry, stirring regularly, until well browned, about 10 minutes. Scrape into a blender jar. Set the pan aside.

Roast the tomato on a baking sheet 4 inches [*10cm*] below a very hot broiler [*grill*] until blackened, about 5 minutes, then flip it and roast the other side; cool, then peel, collecting all the juices with the tomato. Add the tomato to the blender, along with the peanuts, bread, chipotles, drained anchos, allspice and cinnamon. Add 1½ cups [*350ml/12fl oz*] of the broth and blend until smooth, stirring and scraping down the sides of the blender jar, and adding a little more liquid if needed to keep everything moving through the blades. Press the mixture through a medium-mesh strainer into a bowl.

Heat 1 tablespoon of the remaining oil in the pot over medium-high heat. When hot enough to make a drop of the purée sizzle sharply, add it all at once. Stir as the nutty-smelling, ruddy-red amalgamation thickens and darkens for about 5 minutes, then stir in the remaining 2 cups [*500ml/17fl oz*] broth, the wine, vinegar and bay leaves. Partially cover and let gently simmer over medium-low heat for roughly 45 minutes, stirring regularly for the flavours to harmonize. If necessary, thin the sauce with a little more broth to keep it the consistency of a cream soup. Taste and season with salt, about 1½ teaspoons, and the sugar. Cover and keep warm.

Grilling and serving the quail: 30 to 45 minutes before serving, light a gas grill or prepare a charcoal fire and let the coals burn until they are covered with grey ash and medium-hot. Position the grill grate about 8 inches [*20cm*] above the coals and lightly oil.

While the grill heats, lay the quail on a baking sheet. Tie the legs together with kitchen twine, then brush both sides with some of the remaining oil; sprinkle with salt and pepper.

Lay the quail on the hottest portion of the grill, breast-side down. Cover the grill and cook about 8 minutes, checking once or twice to ensure that they are not browning too quickly. Flip the quail and move to a cooler portion of the grill (quail finished over a cooler fire always seem juicier). Cover and continue grilling until the leg meat will separate from the bone quite easily when you squeeze a leg between 2 fingers, 4 to 6 minutes more.

Remove to a plate and keep warm in a low oven while you set up your plates. Ladle a generous ⅓ cup [*85ml/3floz*] of the earthy-coloured sauce on to each of 6 warm dinner plates. Set 2 quail over the sauce. Garnish with chopped peanuts and sprigs of parsley.

Advance preparation
The *mole* may be made up to 5 days ahead, cover and refrigerate. If oil separates from sauce when reheated, either skim it off or blend the sauce in a loosely covered blender. The quail are best cooked just before serving.

David Rosengarten with Joel Dean and Giorgio DeLuca

Provençal Rabbit Stew with Olives and Capers

(The Dean & DeLuca Cookbook)

I blame Beatrix Potter. If she hadn't so thoroughly convinced us that the verminous, destructive rabbit was really a cuddly anthropomorphic bunny we might find delicious and cheap rabbit on menus more often. Sadly, it is only a brave cook who will dish up rabbit for the family. In spite of the fact that we don't seem to eat much of it, it isn't difficult to buy. You can get saddles of rabbit from many butchers and you will certainly find them easier to deal with than the nightmare of jointing a whole animal.

This Provençal rabbit stew uses strong and salty flavourings such as mustard, olives and capers. It makes a good and easy substitute for a dinner-party chicken or beef stew. If you cook it the day before you will give yourself a break and also be able to present a better-tasting dish – stews mature overnight in the fridge. I like to serve it with mashed potatoes mixed with parsnips. Dean & DeLuca isn't just New York's greatest food shop – an extraordinary distinction in the food-obsessed Big Apple. It is also one of the very few food shops anywhere to have put together a first-rate cookbook. I suppose that in these days when ingredients are assuming greater importance, it's not so surprising that a food merchant should produce such a good book.

Serves 6

3 rabbits (about 1.5kg/3lb each)	1 bay leaf
2 tablespoons olive oil, plus additional if necessary for cooking vegetables	1½ teaspoons tomato paste
50g/2oz flour, plus additional if necessary	2 garlic cloves, finely chopped
50ml/2fl oz Dijon mustard	a few pints chicken stock
450g/1lb coarsely chopped onions	1½ teaspoons salt, or to taste
225g/8oz coarsely chopped carrots	450g/1lb fresh plum tomatoes
225ml/8fl oz white wine	350g/12oz brine-cured green olives
1 sprig of thyme	175g/6oz capers
	50g/2oz finely chopped fresh parsley

Preheat oven to 190°C/375°F/Gas Mark 5.

Cut the rabbits in 6 pieces each (the meaty hind legs, the bonier forelegs, plus the centre loin, called *rable* in French, cut in two). Or have your butcher do it for you. In an ovenproof omelette pan wide enough to hold the rabbit pieces in one layer, add the olive oil and place over moderate heat. (If you don't have a pan big enough, you can use 2 and divide the ingredients.)

Put flour in a flat dish. Brush the rabbit pieces with the mustard and then dip into the flour, shaking off any excess. Add the rabbit pieces to the hot oil and cook until golden brown on both sides. Remove rabbit from the pan and set aside.

Add the onions and carrots to the pan (or pans) and cook over moderately high heat until onions are lightly browned. (You may need to add 1 teaspoon of olive oil if the pan is too dry.) Sprinkle the leftover flour, if there is any, into the pan and stir well to blend with the onions. Deglaze the pan with the white wine over high heat and mix well. Add the thyme, bay leaf, tomato paste and garlic and mix well.

Return the rabbit to the pan (or pans). Add enough chicken stock to cover the meat and vegetables by 2.5cm/1 inch (you may combine the stock with water, if desired). Bring to a boil and add the salt. Cover and braise in the oven for 1½ hours, or until the meat is just cooked enough to start falling from the bone.

While the rabbit is cooking, bring a small pot of water to boil. Remove the stems from the tomatoes with the tip of a small knife. Make a small crisscross on the other side of the tomato. Plunge the tomatoes into the boiling water for about 30 seconds, or until skin begins to pull away. Refresh under cold water and remove the peel. Cut in half lengthways and remove the seeds. Chop coarsely and reserve until needed. Rinse the olives in cold water. Reserve.

When the rabbit is ready, carefully remove the pieces from the pan and set aside. Strain the sauce through a colander. Discard the vegetables and herbs.

Return the sauce to the pan and bring to a boil over moderate heat. Add the tomatoes, olives and capers. Reduce the heat and simmer the sauce until it is reduced by about half. Thicken with flour, if desired.

When the sauce is ready, check the seasoning. Add the pieces of rabbit back to the pan to warm. Sprinkle with the chopped parsley and serve right from the pan, on a platter, or divided among 6 individual dinner plates.

Fish and Seafood

Salmon Marinated in Dill

Fish Soup with Croûtons

Salmon Fishcake with Sorrel Sauce

Salmon Wrapped in Courgette Ribbons with Tomato Vinaigrette

Cod with a Parsley Crust

Salt Cod with Tomatoes and Pesto

Vatroushka with Smoked Salmon

Smoked Haddock Pie

Grilled Fish, Romagna Style

Queue de Lotte Rôtie à la Moutarde et Estragon

Peppered Tuna

Roasted Brill with a Brandade of Cod

Filets de Flet à la Moutarde

Oysters with Sausages

Chilled Fish in Escabeche

Yam Pla Muek

Rendez-vous de Fruits-de-Mer à la Crème de Basilic

Mussels with Saffron

Maine Crabmeat Turnovers

Rick Stein

Salmon Marinated in Dill

(Rick Stein's Taste of the Sea)

My West Highland White terrier, Betty, loves smoked salmon. I think it's because when she was a puppy a lot of our friends were getting married and Betty went to a lot of weddings and was fed a lot of smoked salmon sandwiches. I love smoked salmon too, but some that I've tasted isn't good enough for either Betty or me. The buying and eating of smoked salmon has become a fairly chancy enterprise, with a lot of dubious fish on the market. Once all you needed to know was whether you liked your salmon smoked in Scotland or London. Nowadays you have to check its provenance carefully to make sure it really is smoked salmon: a couple of years ago a large consignment was found to be made from frozen rainbow trout shipped in from Chile.

If you are fed up with, or bored by less than the best smoked salmon, the ideal solution is to make your own gravad lax, a rich and buttery cured salmon with dill from Scandinavia which you slice thinly and serve like smoked salmon. It is often served with a dill and mustard sauce. Rick Stein advises that the best cut of fish to use is the middle and suggests that you ask your fishmonger to cut the salmon in half lengthways and remove the bones. Wash and scale the fish before marinating it.

Serves 6

1.25kg/2¹/₂lb fresh salmon
1 large bunch of dill
100g/4oz salt, preferably sea salt

75g/3oz sugar
2 tablespoons white peppercorns, crushed

Place half the fish, skin-side down, in a shallow dish. Roughly chop the dill and mix it with the salt, sugar and crushed peppercorns. Cover the salmon with this dry cure and place the other piece of salmon on top, skin-side up. Cover the fish with aluminium foil or clingfilm and place a plate, slightly bigger than the salmon, on top. Place a weight on top of the plate to press the fish down. Refrigerate for two days, turning the fish about every 12 hours and spooning over the liquid from the salmon. Remember to replace the weight each time.

Remove the salmon from the brine and slice it thinly, like smoked salmon. You can scrape off the dill coating if you like but I think it looks rather nice to have a green line of dill on each slice.

Rick Stein

Fish Soup with Croûtons

(Rick Stein's Taste of the Sea)

Rick Stein is Britain's best and best-known writer about fish cookery. I love his impeccable yet rough and ready recipes. This one begins with typical gusto as he specifies 1.75 kilos of fish – so no chasing around searching for some arcane species, instead just get what looks best on the fishmonger's ice. Rick writes that any fish will do except 'oily ones like mackerel and herring. You can also use prawns and other shellfish scraps, like lobster, crab, langoustine and shrimps or mussels'. I suggest that you ask your fishmonger to fillet the fish and give you the bones and trimmings for stock. To make the stock, simply put the bones, heads, etc. in a large pan and cover with 2.25 litres/4 pints of water. Bring to the boil and simmer very gently for 20 minutes, then strain through a muslin-lined sieve. Return the stock to the pan with a chopped-up onion, leek, carrot and celery stick, then simmer again for 45 minutes before straining to use in the soup.

If you don't have the conical strainer which Rick suggests, just push the purée through a sieve. I don't have enough self-control to eat fish soup as a first course: I want seconds and thirds and so prefer to eat it for supper.

Serves 6–8

1.75kg/4lb fish
225g/8oz prawns in the shell
2.25 litres/4 pints water
150ml/¼ pint olive oil
175g/6oz onion, roughly chopped
175g/6oz celery, roughly chopped
175g/6oz leek, roughly chopped
175g/6oz Florence fennel, roughly chopped
5 garlic cloves, sliced
juice of 1 orange plus 5cm (2 inch) piece peel
400g/14oz tin of tomatoes
1 red pepper, sliced

1 fresh or dried bay leaf
1 sprig of thyme
¼ teaspoon saffron
a large pinch of cayenne pepper
salt and freshly ground black pepper
For the croûtons:
1 baguette
olive oil
2 garlic cloves, peeled
50g/2oz freshly grated Parmesan
2 tablespoons *Rouille* (see below)

Fillet all the fish and use the heads and bones to make a fish stock with the 2.25 litres/4 pints of water.

Heat the olive oil in a large pan and add the onion, celery, leek, fennel and garlic. Cook gently for about 20 minutes without colouring until the vegetables are very soft. Add the orange peel, tomatoes, red pepper, bay leaf, thyme, saffron, prawns and fish fillets. Cook briskly, stirring, then add the stock and orange juice. Bring to the boil and simmer for 40 minutes.

Liquidize the soup in a liquidizer or food processor, then pass it through a conical strainer, pushing it through with the back of a ladle to extract all the juices. Return to the heat and season with salt, pepper and cayenne. The soup should be a little on the salty side, with a subtle but noticeable hint of cayenne.

To make the croûtons, thinly slice the baguette then fry in olive oil. When cool enough to handle, rub the croûtons with garlic. Serve the soup, Parmesan and *rouille* separately. The idea is that each person spreads some *rouille* on to the croûtons, floats them in the soup and sprinkles them with Parmesan.

Rouille

25g/1 oz dry bread soaked in fish stock
3 garlic cloves
1 egg yolk

2 tablespoons *harissa*
1/4 teaspoon salt
250ml/8fl oz olive oil

Put all the ingredients except the olive oil in a food processor and blend. Then gradually pour in the oil until it is incorporated into the egg yolks.

A. A. Gill and Mark Hix

Salmon Fishcake with Sorrel Sauce

(The Ivy)

The fishcake: a simple, even homely dish that can cover a multitude of gastronomic sins. Kitchen slobs make their fishcakes with tinned fish or scrappy bits of leftovers; good cooks, as always, take care. When I was little, fishcakes in Boston were made with salt cod and served up with huge plates of chips and a blob of Heinz ketchup. Thanks to two of London's best and most enduringly fashionable restaurants – Le Caprice and the Ivy – this once-lowly dish pops up on high-rent menus all over town. It is, as A. A. Gill writes in his book *The Ivy: The Restaurant and its Recipes*, 'the most copied dish on the menu'. It first appeared at Le Caprice and Gill goes on to say that the owners, Chris Corbin and Jeremy King, 'didn't realize quite how popular [the dish was] until they dropped it. The menu had to be reprinted. There are customers who still order nothing else'. I guess the stroke of genius in this recipe from Mark Hix, chef at the Ivy, is seasoning the fishcakes with ketchup, mustard and anchovy essence. The sorrel sauce is delicious but I still prefer them with ketchup.

Makes 8

1.5kg/3lb spinach, picked over, washed and
  dried

For the fishcakes:

650g/1lb 7oz dry mashed potato, no cream or
  butter added

650g/1lb 7oz salmon fillet, poached in fish
  stock and flaked

2 tablespoons tomato ketchup

2 teaspoons anchovy essence

3 teaspoons English mustard

salt and freshly ground black pepper

For the sauce:

500ml/17fl oz strong fish stock

50g/2oz butter

25g/1oz flour

50ml/2fl oz white wine

250ml/8fl oz double cream

15g/¹⁄₂oz fresh sorrel, shredded

salt and pepper

To make the fishcakes, mix together the potato, half the poached salmon, the ketchup, anchovy essence, mustard and seasoning until it is smooth. Fold in the rest of the salmon. Mould the mixture into 8 round cakes and refrigerate.

To make the sauce, bring the fish stock to the boil in a thick-bottomed pan. In another pan melt the butter and stir in the flour. Cook very slowly over a low heat for 30 seconds, then gradually whisk in the fish stock. Pour in the white wine and simmer gently for 30 minutes until the sauce has thickened. Add the cream and reduce the sauce until it is of a thick pouring consistency, then put in the sorrel and season.

Preheat the oven to 200°C/400°F/Gas Mark 6. Lightly flour the fishcakes and fry them until they are coloured on both sides, then bake them for 10–15 minutes.

Heat a large saucepan over a medium flame, add the spinach, season it lightly and cover tightly with a lid. Cook for 3–4 minutes, stirring occasionally, until the leaves are tender. Drain in a colander.

Put some spinach on each plate, then a fishcake and pour over the sauce. Serve immediately.

Paul and Jeanne Rankin

Salmon Wrapped in Courgette Ribbons with Tomato Vinaigrette

(Gourmet Ireland Two)

Paul and Jeanne Rankin own a restaurant in downtown Belfast called Roscoff, after the little port in Brittany. The first time I was taken there for lunch I was overwhelmed. Not only was this by far the best cooking in Northern Ireland, it was also a restaurant that could have stood the competition of the London restaurant scene. It's gratifying that through the politically bad times and good times in Belfast, Roscoff has flourished thanks to a devoted clientele and to the Rankins' creativity and determination. As cooks, Paul and Jeanne have always been very aware of fashion – they have travelled, cooked and eaten around the world – but most importantly they have shown a deep respect for the produce and culinary traditions of Paul's native Ireland. Salmon wrapped in courgette ribbons sounds fussy and even slightly ridiculous; in fact it's a glamorous and fairly easy barbecue dish which packs a punch thanks to its cracked pepper vinaigrette.

Serves 6

675g/1¹/₂lb fresh salmon, skinned and boned
3 medium courgettes
salt and freshly ground black pepper
2 tablespoons light olive oil

For the vinaigrette:

4 plum tomatoes, skinned, deseeded and
**   diced**
50g/2oz fresh basil leaves, chopped
100ml/3¹/₂fl oz extra virgin olive oil
1 tablespoon lemon juice
¹/₄ teaspoon salt
¹/₄ teaspoon cracked black pepper

Preheat the barbecue or grill. Soak six 15cm/6 inch wooden skewers in water for 1 hour.

Cut the salmon fillet into 2.5cm/1 inch dice or into 24 even pieces. With a potato peeler, peel 13cm/5 inch ribbons off the courgettes. Carefully wrap each cube of salmon with a strip of courgette. Slice and skewer each piece as it is prepared, allowing about 4 pieces of salmon per skewer. Season each one with a little salt and pepper, brush with a little olive oil and cook on the barbecue for about 5 minutes, turning occasionally, until firm and cooked.

While the salmon is cooking, mix all the ingredients for the vinaigrette in a small bowl, then divide between warmed plates. When the salmon is ready, lift the brochettes on to the plates and serve immediately.

Cod with a Parsley Crust

(Rhodes Around Britain)

Although he first came to prominence cooking at the Capital Hotel in Knightsbridge before moving on to the Greenhouse in Mayfair, Gary Rhodes's cheerfully demotic style is not at all what you would expect from a chef used to the high-rent districts of town. A series of television programmes and commercials have made Gary the people's chef and he has been a significant force in encouraging cooks to re-examine and reinvent traditional British cookery. He and other young chefs have helped to elevate the once ubiquitous and rather unloved cod to dizzying culinary heights. It is a magnificent fish to eat, snow white and just starting to flake as it reaches the perfect stage of cooking. In this recipe, which owes its ancestry to an *haute cuisine* classic, Veal Orloff, Gary puts a herby butter and breadcrumb paste over the fish, grills it and then finishes the dish in a hot oven. He serves it with lemon butter sauce and mashed potatoes; I like it with spinach or a green salad.

Serves 4

75g/3oz unsalted butter

2 shallots, finely chopped

4 tablespoons chopped fresh parsley

½ large white sliced loaf, crusts removed and crumbed

salt and freshly ground white pepper

4 cod fillet pieces, each about 175–225g/6–8oz

Preheat the grill to medium, preheat the oven to 180–200°C/350–400°F/Gas Mark 4–6, and butter and season a flameproof dish.

Melt the butter with the chopped shallots, which should just soften them, then remove from the heat. Add the chopped parsley to the breadcrumbs and season with salt and pepper. Gradually mix this with the shallot butter to form a light paste. Place the fish on the prepared dish and cover each cod fillet with the parsley crust. Cook the cod under the grill, not too near the heat. It will take about 8–10 minutes. As the crust slowly colours, the fish will be cooking. When the fish under the crust turns opaque and milky and the crust is golden brown, it is ready. Finish in the preheated oven for a few minutes to make sure the fish is completely cooked.

Nigel Slater

Salt Cod with Tomatoes and Pesto

(Real Good Food)

In the State House, as we call the Capitol building in Boston, Massachusetts, a gilt wood carving of a codfish hangs in the House of Representatives. It is known as the Sacred Cod and pays tribute to the abundance of cod off the New England coast, which helped to build the fortune of many a Massachusetts family. The cod were caught, salted and then shipped back to Europe. In the days before refrigeration, salting and drying were the only ways that fish could be preserved. This food was especially important in Portugal, Spain and Italy – countries with hot weather and big Catholic populations who had many meat-free days (including every Friday) in their calendar. Salt cod isn't eaten much in New England these days, except as fishcakes, but it remains popular in both Spain and Portugal. I feel it is much maligned because it looks so dreadful when you buy it and smells so frightful when you cook it. But it is wonderful, just slightly fibrous and with a stimulating salty tang, as you would expect. I once ate three courses of salt cod in a Barcelona restaurant which serves nothing but.

This recipe is exemplary Nigel Slater: pragmatic, full of the rough and tumble of real cooking and nicely simplifying, without degrading, the often long and tricky traditional salt cod recipes. Before you start cooking remember that you need to soak the fish for at least 24 hours, changing the water frequently. The result as Nigel Slater describes it is 'a deeply savoury dish best accompanied with unbuttered, unskinned boiled potatoes and a little more wine than usual'.

Serves 2

2 steaks of salt cod about 200g/7oz each,
  soaked in several changes of water for at
  least 24 hours
olive oil
flour
1 clove of garlic, peeled

2 small, dried chillies
4 tomatoes, deseeded and chopped (you can
  skin them if you wish, it makes little
  difference here)
2 tablespoons pesto sauce from a jar
a small glass of white wine

Pour 4 tablespoons of olive oil into an ovenproof dish and place the soaked cod steaks skin-side up in the oil. Set aside for at least half an hour.

Preheat the oven to 200°C/400°F/Gas Mark 6. Put a layer of flour on a flat plate and press the cod steaks into it so that they retain some of the flour. Pour the oil in which the fish has been sitting into a shallow-sided pan and fry the fish steaks on both sides till golden and crisp.

Lift the fish back into the ovenproof dish. Wipe the flour and oil from the inside of the shallow pan – there is no need to be too scrupulous about this – and add a little more oil. Add the clove of garlic roughly crushed (you can squash it flat with the blade of a knife) and the chillies, crushed. Warm the oil over a medium heat until the garlic turns pale gold, then add the tomatoes, cook for 2 minutes, then stir in the pesto and the wine. Allow to bubble for a couple of minutes then season with freshly ground black pepper.

Slosh the sauce – actually it is more of a gunge – around the fish and cook in the pre-heated oven for 15 minutes, a little longer if the steaks are really thick. When the sauce is bubbling and the fish cooked right through it is ready. Serve simply with boiled rice or, better still, plain boiled potatoes.

Karen Craig and Seva Novgorodsev

Vatroushka with Smoked Salmon

(The Cooking of Russia)

The old Russian Tea Room (I say old because a more lavish establishment under new ownership has opened), right next door to Carnegie Hall in Manhattan, was a glitzy, show-business watering hole decorated *à la* Winter Palace and dishing up Russian food of varying quality. I used to be taken there by my Russian Uncle Max, and developed a taste for *blini, pierogi, pelmeni* etc. from an early age. When I first visited Russia, in pre-Glasnost days, the food was not as good as at the Russian Tea Room; in fact it was everything you would expect of a totalitarian cuisine – grey and scanty. There was plenty of cheap caviar, but not much else. Without making an ideological point I can fairly say that socialist revolutions tend to regard good cooking as 'bourgeois' and contemptible. Maybe new Russia will pay more attention to its native culinary traditions.

Russians are fond of savoury pastries, many of which are made with a yeast dough, although Karen Craig and Seva Novgorodsev suggest that you can get away with using frozen puff pastry. This *vatroushka* is really just a more interesting smoked salmon quiche, notable for the use of *smetana*, a pleasantly sour cultured dairy product which was named after the 19th-century Czech composer Bedrich Smetana. It is surprisingly easy to find, but if you can't get it, just substitute a mixture of half double cream and half soured cream. You can eat this flan cold, but it is better warm as a smart first course or the centrepiece of a casual lunch.

Serves 8

butter for greasing
450g/1lb puff pastry
flour for rolling
For the filling:
350g/12oz smoked salmon, cut into thin strips

6 eggs
500ml/18fl oz smetana
a bunch of fresh dill, chopped
pepper

Grease a large 25–30cm/10–12 inch round baking tin with a removable base. Roll the pastry out on a floured surface into a circle slightly larger than the tin and 1.25cm/½ inch thick. Line the tin with the pastry. Prick the bottom with a fork. Chill for 20 minutes.

Preheat the oven to 240°C/475°F/Gas Mark 9.

Place the smoked salmon strips on top of the pastry.

Beat the eggs in a large bowl until frothy, then beat in the smetana. Add the dill and pepper to taste. Pour this mixture over the salmon.

Place in the oven and bake for 15 minutes; then turn the oven down to 220°C/425°F/Gas Mark 7. Bake for 25–30 minutes, checking after 15 minutes and turning if necessary, until golden and cooked through.

Allow to cool for 5 minutes, then place on a warmed serving dish. Garnish with more dill and serve immediately.

Arabella Boxer

Smoked Haddock Pie

(First Slice Your Cookbook)

So many years, so many cookbooks yet *First Slice Your Cookbook* remains the cleverest ever. As a package it is as simple and elegant as the recipes it contains. Each 'page' is a series of cards that flip over to enable you to mix starters, main courses and puddings at leisure until you come up with your ideal dinner-party menu. Having chosen your three courses you can then keep them all open at the same time. It is one of the icons of sixties graphic design and remains a tribute to the talent of the late Mark Boxer – witty cartoonist, sometime editor of the *Tatler*, one of the fathers of the Sunday colour supplement and ex-husband of Arabella. This recipe is an exemplar of Arabella's style, which I suppose in this case you might define as classic British with a spin. Some things about the recipe confound me. I don't like either cheese or tomatoes with fish but here they blend together deliciously and harmoniously. I like my fish pie to have a thick mashed potato top but in this recipe there's no potato. I emphatically agree with Arabella Boxer that smoked haddock is the finest fish for a pie, especially if you take the trouble to buy pale and creamy-looking *undyed* fish and not that stuff that's the same colour as a JCB. I think that Arabella Boxer's description of this as 'a good supper dish as it can be made in advance' is altogether too modest. I wouldn't hesitate to dish this up at the grandest dinner party, and if you feel it's too humble a dish just dust off your most expensive bottles of white Burgundy to raise the tone.

2 large smoked haddock
4 eggs
4 tomatoes
675g/1¹/₂lb spinach (or 450g/1lb frozen leaf spinach)
salt, pepper
1 tablespoon butter

For the cheese sauce:
2 tablespoons butter
2 tablespoons flour
300ml/¹/₂ pint milk
salt, pepper
50g/2oz grated cheese

Bring a large pan of water to the boil. Cut the fish in 8 pieces. When the water boils, put in the fish, cover, and remove from heat. After 10 minutes, drain and cool fish. Remove skin and bone, and flake it. Hard-boil the eggs. Cool, shell and slice thickly. Peel the tomatoes after dipping in boiling water, and slice them.

Butter a soufflé dish. Cook the spinach and drain, forcing out all the water with a wooden spoon. Season well and toss in a little butter. Put the spinach in the bottom of the dish, then the flaked fish, the sliced eggs, and finally the sliced tomatoes, seasoning well after each layer.

Make the cheese sauce. Pour over the dish, shaking well so that it penetrates. Put in a slow oven for ¹/₂ hour. It can be kept hot indefinitely or made in advance and reheated gently. Serve with a green salad.

Marcella Hazan

Grilled Fish, Romagna Style

(The Essentials of Classic Italian Cooking)

The North End of Boston is one of the oldest Italian neighbourhoods in America. When I was little we often went out to dinner there. In the Fifties and early Sixties Italian cooking in America (particularly in restaurant-filled areas like the North End) was dominated by what is now rather disparagingly known as 'red sauce cooking', a fairly bastardized form of Neapolitan food in which everything seemed to be served up with an unexciting, thick tomato sauce. Then Marcella Hazan came along and, more than anyone else, she taught Americans what 'real' Italian cooking was about. Her exact, didactic recipes meant that even Great Aunt Minnie from Sioux City could learn to cook like a Tuscan mamma. Incidentally, just when the Land of the Free has embraced polenta and balsamic vinegar with a vengeance, there has been something of a red sauce revival, with a number of hip Fifties-style Italian restaurants opening up.

The best way to cook fish is the simplest and I feel there's no better method than grilling. Marcella Hazan's technique isn't often seen in restaurants and works best with small whole fish such as bass, bream or mackerel. You just briefly marinate the fish in a mixture of oil, lemon juice, rosemary and dried breadcrumbs and sling it under a grill. If possible make your own breadcrumbs. Put some slices of bread in a warm oven for a few hours then crush them in a food processor. They store well in a screwtop jar. If you must buy readymade, please avoid the bright orange ones.

Serves 4 or more

1.25–1.5kg/2¹/₂–3lb whole fish, gutted and
    scaled, or fish steaks
salt
freshly ground black pepper
4 tablespoons extra virgin olive oil
2 tablespoons freshly squeezed lemon juice

a small sprig fresh rosemary or ¹/₂ teaspoon
    very finely chopped dried leaves
6 tablespoons fine, dry, plain breadcrumbs
a small branch of fresh bay leaves or several
    dried leaves, optional
a charcoal or wood-burning grill, optional

Wash the fish or the fish steaks in cold water, then thoroughly pat dry with kitchen
paper.

Sprinkle the fish liberally with salt and pepper on both sides, put it on a large platter
and add the olive oil, lemon juice and rosemary. Turn the fish two or three times to coat
it well. Add the breadcrumbs, turning the fish once or twice again until it has an even
coating of oil-soaked breadcrumbs. Marinate for 1 to 2 hours at room temperature,
turning and basting the fish from time to time.

If using charcoal or wood, light the charcoal in time for it to form white ash before
cooking, or the wood long enough in advance to reduce it to hot embers. If using an
indoor gas or electric grill, preheat it at least 15 minutes before you are ready to cook.

Place the fish 10–12cm/4–5 inches from the source of heat. Do not discard its
marinade. If cooking on charcoal or with wood, throw the bay leaves into the fire,
otherwise omit. Grill on both sides until done. Depending on the thickness of the fish
steaks or the size of the whole fish, it may take between 5 and 15 minutes. While
cooking on an open grill, baste the side away from the fire with the marinade. Serve
piping hot from the grill.

Raymond Blanc

Queue de Lotte Rôtie à la Moutarde et Estragon

Roasted Fillet of Monkfish with a Mustard and Tarragon Sauce

(Cooking for Friends)

Monkfish is frightful to look at, tiresome to clean and delicious to eat. It was for many years a cheap fish that British fishermen routinely threw away or attempted to flog as ersatz scampi, even though its culinary qualities were much appreciated in both France and Italy. Smart British diners discovered it in the early Eighties and it is now as expensive a fish as you can buy. Amongst its great merits are firm flesh and no bones, so it appeals greatly to the more timid fisheaters. At the fishmonger's you will rarely see it whole – the huge and menacing head is too frightening to entice customers. When you buy the monkfish tails for this recipe, ask your fishmonger to remove the thin, dark membrane around them, as this is difficult to do at home. And while you're at it, also ask him to remove the 'backbone' (cartilage, really) and you will be left with two fillets. Some supermarkets sell the fish cleaned and ready to cook.

Raymond Blanc's recipe is the best way to cook monkfish and also one of the simplest: basically you just sear it (this caramelizes the outer flesh and intensifies the flavour) and then finish off the cooking in the oven. If you like your monkfish unadorned, just add a squeeze of lemon. For a more sophisticated dish, go all the way with Raymond's excellent mustard and tarragon sauce – something that you'd typically find served with rabbit, but which is also superb with monkfish. For some reason, sauced fish dishes are often served with plain boiled rice or (to my mind even more boring) steamed potatoes. I'd go for wild rice or Pierre Franey's Riz Arménien (see page 54).

Serves 4

1kg/2¼lb monkfish on the bone	chopped bones and trimmings from the fish
2 tablespoons olive oil	(throw the dark skin away)
salt and freshly ground pepper	*To finish the sauce:*
lemon juice	2 tablespoons whipping cream
For the sauce base:	1 teaspoon mustard seeds (or 1 teaspoon
2 shallots, peeled and chopped	*moutarde à l'ancienne*)
2 large teaspoons unsalted butter	40g/1½oz cold unsalted butter, diced
100ml/3½fl oz white wine vinegar	12 tarragon leaves
100ml/3½fl oz white wine	5g/¼oz chopped chives
150ml/¼ pint water	1 teaspoon lemon juice

Preheat the oven to 200°C/400°F/Gas Mark 6.

Preparing the monkfish: peel off the dark skin from the fish and discard. Trim the outer skin and reserve for the stock. Bone out the fish, and chop the bone.

You will have two fillets of about 350g/12oz each, and the trimmings and chopped bone should weigh in at about 200g/7oz.

Tie the fillets so they keep their shape during cooking. Place on a tray, cover with clingfilm and refrigerate.

Preparing the sauce base: place the shallots in a saucepan and sweat in the butter for 2–3 minutes. Add the white wine vinegar and reduce completely. Add the white wine and reduce by half then add the water and the chopped bones and trimmings. Bring to the boil, skim and simmer for 10 minutes. Strain into a small casserole and reserve.

Cooking the monkfish fillets: sear the fillets all over in the hot olive oil for 1 minute. Season with salt and pepper, then cook in the preheated oven for 7 minutes.

Remove from the oven, spoon out any fat and reserve the fillets, loosely covered with aluminium foil, in a warm place.

Finishing the sauce: during the cooking of the monkfish, bring the sauce base stock to the boil. Add the cream and mustard, then gradually whisk in the cold diced butter. Add the tarragon and chives. Taste, season and keep warm.

Finishing and serving the dish: remove the string from the monkfish fillets. Reheat in the oven for 2 minutes. Cut six medallions from each fillet and season with salt and pepper. Add a dash of lemon juice, arrange on warm plates (three per plate), and pour the sauce over. Serve to your guests.

Julee Rosso

Peppered Tuna

(Fresh Start)

This is a witty modern parody of the classic *steak au poivre*. I don't really know who came up with the idea, although I first ate tuna cooked this way at Alastair Little's restaurant. The cooking is as straightforward as can be: coat the tuna with pepper and grill it. I wouldn't bother cracking my own peppercorns as Julee Rosso does; you can buy perfectly good cracked ones in jars. For a little variation, though, you could mix in some Szechuan peppercorns, which you will have to crush yourself with a mortar and pestle.

This recipe was written before ridged cast iron grill pans became so popular and I would just slap the tuna into a very hot grill pan. Tuna cooks quickly and tastes best when underdone, so you'll have to keep an eye on it. Rosso's

sauce is simple and good and, yes, red wine does go with fish, but I usually make this without any sauce at all – just a squeeze of lemon juice on the tuna steaks.

A decent fishmonger should be able to get yellowfin tuna for you but any other variety will do. If you have only ever seen tuna in steaks on fishmonger's ice or in tins on a shelf you won't know what a magnificent fish it is. These cousins of the mackerel are fast, aggressive and big: some species weigh over half a ton.

Like so many others, this dish goes well with mashed potatoes: try grating some lemon zest into the mash when serving it with fish. It's also good served (without the sauce) on top of a bed of rocket salad that has been lightly dressed with olive oil and lemon.

Serves 4

2–4 tablespoons cracked black peppercorns
  (see Note below)
Four 6-ounce [*175g*] yellowfin tuna steaks
salt to taste

2 tablespoons [*25g/1oz*] unsalted butter
¼ cup [*4 tablespoons*] chopped garlic
2 tablespoons chopped fresh tarragon
2 cups [*500ml/17fl oz*] dry red wine

Preheat the broiler [*grill*] or prepare a charcoal or gas grill.

Press the cracked pepper into both sides of the tuna and season with a little salt. Broil or grill 4 inches [*10cm*] from the heat for 4 to 6 minutes on each side, until opaque throughout (or rare in the centre, if you prefer). Cover and keep warm.

In a small skillet [*frying pan*], melt the butter over medium-high heat. Add the garlic and cook for 2 to 3 minutes, until lightly browned. Add the tarragon and wine, raise the heat and boil for 4 to 5 minutes, until reduced to ½ cup [*120ml/4fl oz*]. Spoon the sauce over the tuna and serve immediately.

Note

To crack whole peppercorns, place them on a cutting board and, with the broad side of a chef's knife positioned on the peppercorns, pound the side of the knife several times with your open hand until the peppercorns crack into coarse pieces.

Roasted Brill with a Brandade of Cod

(A Passion for Flavour)

For cutting-edge cuisine – technically demanding, innovative and packed with punchy flavours – Gordon Ramsay is hard to beat on either side of the Atlantic. An ex-footballer with a small, heavily booked-up London restaurant, he is an extraordinarily exacting cook. This is the sort of recipe you shouldn't even be attempting unless you are the type of enthusiast who has a ready supply of veal stock at home. If you want to blow away your friends with restaurant-style food, follow the recipe to a T and see how many will subsequently be reluctant to invite you round. If you feel life is too short, do as I do and simplify: I just make the brandade (four times the quantity specified in the recipe) and serve it with a green salad, spinach or French beans.

You may be familiar with brandade, which is a hypnotically garlic-laden mixture of salt cod and mashed potato. I love it, but preparing it is an ordeal which for weeks afterwards has people sniffing the air and asking, 'Salt cod?' Gordon Ramsay's slightly more refined version uses fresh cod roasted to intensify its flavour. Don't pour all the milk in at once as the amount you need will depend on the type of potato you use – some varieties absorb more than others. The texture of the finished brandade should be spoonable but firm; definitely not runny.

Whether you go the whole hog on this recipe or not it is worth making some of Gordon Ramsay's shallot confit: just stew finely chopped shallots very slowly in oil until soft and lightly caramelized. Make a lot, cool it and keep it in the fridge. It's very handy for adding to all sorts of dishes.

Serves 4

1 tablespoon olive oil

200g/7oz cod fillets, skinned and cut into chunks

150g/5oz potatoes, peeled and diced

500ml/17fl oz milk

1 clove garlic, peeled and crushed

2 tablespoons double cream

2 teaspoons chopped parsley

For the sauce:

2 tablespoons Shallot Confit

3 tablespoons Madeira

2 teaspoons sherry vinegar

400ml/14fl oz veal stock

For the brill and garnish:

200g/7oz young spinach leaves

25g/1oz butter

200g/7oz asparagus tips

2 tablespoons olive oil, plus extra for serving

2 x 300g/11oz brill fillets, cut lengthways into 4 long fillets

sea salt and freshly ground black pepper

For the brandade, heat the oil in a heavy-based pan. 'Roast' the cod on the top of the stove until just cooked and golden. Remove, flake and cool.

Cook the potatoes in the milk along with the garlic and some salt and pepper until soft but not broken down. Drain through a colander set over a bowl, reserving the milk. Mash the potatoes in a large bowl until smooth, then slowly mix in the reserved milk and the cream, beating until you have a creamy paste. You may not need all the milk, but do use all the cream.

Using a spatula, fold the flaked cod gently into the potato, keeping the fish as flaky as possible. Season, mix in the parsley and set aside.

To make the sauce, cook the Shallot Confit and Madeira in a small saucepan until the liquid is reduced by half. Deglaze with the sherry vinegar and cook again for a few seconds until reduced a little, then pour in the veal stock. Boil until reduced by half. Check the seasoning and set aside in a warm place.

Blanch the spinach in lightly salted boiling water until just wilted, drain, return to the pan, off the heat, with a little of the butter. Blanch the asparagus tips until just tender and return to their pan with the remaining butter.

To cook the brill, heat the oil in a heavy-based sauté pan set over a medium heat. Add the fillets and cook for about 2 minutes on each side. Season well, remove and keep warm.

Reheat the brandade over a low heat in a saucepan. Arrange the spinach in a mound on each warmed plate. Place a fillet of brill on top of each mound. Reheat the asparagus if necessary and arrange around the edges. *Nappe* (coat) the fish with the sauce, trickling a little over the vegetables as well. Spoon one-quarter of the brandade on top of each fillet. Finally, dribble over a little olive oil and serve.

Pierre Franey

Filets de Flet à la Moutarde
Broiled Flounder Fillets with Mustard

[60-Minute Gourmet]

Pierre Franey is the most sound and companionable chef to guide the perplexed cook in a hurry. I love his description of first tasting this dish, when he was served it by friends: 'It was a simple dish of broiled fish but the flavour was a bit piquant and there was a golden brown topping. The only two ingredients of which I was absolutely certain were, in addition to the fish and the parsley garnish, the flavour of lemon and mustard.'

Like Franey, when I first ate this dish I searched for a clever explanation: was the fish somehow glazed with hollandaise? It is altogether uncomplicated. Just paint some fish fillets with mustard mayonnaise and pop them under the grill. That is more or less it. Franey's recipe calls for flounder – an American flat fish – but I've cooked this in Britain with all sorts of fillets: Dover sole, halibut tail, plaice, lemon sole. It is one of the best ways there is to cook fish and produces a dish of a complexity and sophistication that is inversely proportional to the effort put into it. What more could a cook ask for?

Serves 4

8 small, skinless, boneless flounder fillets, about 1 pound [450g]
salt and freshly ground pepper to taste
1 tablespoon peanut, vegetable or corn oil
2 tablespoons mayonnaise, preferably homemade although bottled mayonnaise may be used

1 tablespoon imported mustard such as Dijon or Düsseldorf
2 teaspoons finely chopped parsley
4 lemon or lime wedges

Preheat the broiler [grill] to high. Place the fillet halves on a flat surface. Sprinkle with salt and pepper and brush with oil.

Arrange the fillets on a baking sheet or dish. Blend the mayonnaise, mustard and parsley. Brush it evenly over the fillets.

Place the fillets under the broiler, about three or four inches [7.5–8cm] from the source of heat. Broil [grill] about 1 minute or until golden brown on top and the fish is just cooked through. Serve with lemon or lime wedges.

Edouard de Pomiane

Oysters with Sausages

(Cooking in Ten Minutes)

A French-born Pole who died in 1964, de Pomiane is the sharpest and wittiest cookbook writer of the century. His recipes have the sort of edge and concision that you find in classic Hollywood scripts. Whenever I read one of de Pomiane's recipes I imagine Groucho Marx reciting it. His *Cooking in Ten Minutes* is probably the best cookbook you could ever give to someone who likes to eat well but can't really cook. It is very much a survival handbook for people who feel that cooking is less about fancy technique than about careful shopping.

Oysters and sausages make an unusual, though not fanciful, combination. You will find them served together sometimes in Bordeaux and I suppose that in theory and taste the dish isn't that far away from our more familiar combination of oysters and bacon.

Fry some chipolata sausages. Serve them very hot on a dish and on a second dish a dozen oysters.

Alternate the sensations. Burn your mouth with a crackling sausage. Soothe your burns with a cool oyster. Continue until all the sausages and oysters have disappeared.

White wine, of course.

Chilled Fish in Escabeche

(Sunset Magazine)

Sunset is a venerable glossy magazine about the good life of the American Southwest. Years before Southwestern cooking became fashionable with East Coast yuppies, *Sunset*'s cookbooks were on the kitchen shelves of American foodies. Their deadpan reliability has brought what they call 'Mexican-Old West' flavours into many households.

Don't confuse this recipe with the similar-sounding South American ceviche, in which you 'cook' chunks of raw fish by marinating them in lime juice flavoured with onions, chillies and coriander. In escabeche the fish is fried first and then infused with a vinegar marinade. You may have had a similar dish around Venice where they make fish *in saor* – fried and then pickled to produce a piquant sweet and sour quality.

Fish in Escabeche keeps well in the fridge and you can serve it as a first course or as a main course, dressed up with some black olives, wedges of hard-boiled egg and slices of boiled potato.

Serves 6–8

4 teaspoons Escabeche Paste (see below)

1/3 cup [85ml/3fl oz] olive oil or salad oil

2 cloves garlic, minced or pressed

1/3 cup [85ml/3fl oz] each orange juice and white wine vinegar

2/3 cup [175ml/6fl oz] regular-strength chicken broth

2 teaspoons sugar

2 dry bay leaves

about 2 pounds [900g] fish fillets such as red snapper or sole; or 2 pounds [900g] pieces of swordfish, halibut or shark, 1 inch [2.5cm] thick

1 large mild red onion, sliced and separated into rings

1 can (4oz [100g]) whole green chillies, drained and deseeded

spinach leaves

1/2 cup [15g/1/2oz] fresh cilantro [coriander] leaves

Prepare Escabeche Paste. Heat 1 tablespoon of the oil in a pan over medium heat; add Escabeche Paste and garlic. Cook, stirring, for 1 minute. Gradually stir in orange juice, vinegar, broth, sugar and bay leaves; bring to a boil over high heat. Then reduce heat and keep warm.

Fold thin fish fillets in half to form 1 inch [2.5cm] thick pieces. Heat 3 more tablespoons oil in a wide frying pan over medium heat. Add fish in a single layer; cook, turning once, until fish is golden brown on outside and flakes when prodded with a fork (4 to 5 minutes per side). Repeat to cook remaining fish, adding more oil as needed.

Arrange fish in a 9 inch [23cm] square baking dish; top with onion. Spoon warm escabeche mixture over fish. Cover and refrigerate for at least 8 hours or until next day; spoon marinade over fish several times.

Lay chillies flat on a rimmed platter; surround with spinach. Set fish on chillies; top with onion and cilantro. Spoon marinade over all.

Escabeche Paste

Stir together 8 cloves garlic, minced or pressed; 1 teaspoon each ground allspice, ground cloves, ground cumin and ground coriander; 1 1/2 teaspoons ground cinnamon; 3/4 teaspoon coarsely ground pepper; 2 teaspoons dried oregano leaves; 1/4 teaspoon ground red pepper (cayenne); and 2 tablespoons each orange juice and white wine vinegar. Use, or cover and refrigerate for up to 2 weeks.

Sri Owen

Yam Pla Muek
Squid Salad

(Healthy Thai Cooking)

I was a little suspicious of the book in which this recipe appears, since it has two fashionable buzzwords in the title – 'healthy' and 'Thai'. But Sri Owen is one of the most practical, reliable cookery writers around and she has succeeded in producing recipes that are full of authentic flavours yet lighter than average. This one is especially good.

Squid is easy to buy but a total pain in the neck to clean. Ask your fishmonger to do it for you. If you have never cooked squid before you will be delighted at how simple it is, provided you follow Sri's advice: 'Squid pieces must be cooked for only 3–4 minutes, whether they are fried or poached. If you overrun that time, the squid will need to be cooked for 40 minutes or longer to make it tender again.' Strange but true. I cooked squid for the first time only recently and now cook it as often as any other seafood. It is so quick and easy, it's almost cooked before you can say knife.

A few words about ingredients. Red bird chillies are extremely hot so use them sparingly and be sure to wash your hands thoroughly after handling them – otherwise their volatile juice may end up where it shouldn't be if you happen to rub your eyes or scratch your nose. *Nam pla* is the ubiquitous seasoning of Thailand, used instead of (and sometimes alongside) salt or soy sauce. It belongs to a long and widespread tradition of condiments that are sometimes known as rotten-fish sauces. The most famous was liquamen, used by the ancient Romans: you probably have a bottle of its modern descendant lurking in a kitchen cupboard – Worcestershire sauce, which is also made with anchovies (although not rotten ones).

Serves 4–6 as a first course

675g/1¹/₂lb small squid, cleaned
900ml/1¹/₂ pints water
¹/₂ teaspoon salt
1 cucumber, halved lengthwise, seeds scooped out and flesh cut into thin half-moon shapes

For the dressing:
juice of 1 lime
1 tablespoon *nam pla* fish sauce
1 tablespoon light soy sauce
2 teaspoons rice vinegar
1–3 small red bird chillies, finely chopped
2 shallots, very finely sliced
2 teaspoons caster sugar
4 tablespoons warm water
1 tablespoon chopped coriander leaves
1 tablespoon chopped basil leaves

Start by mixing all the ingredients for the dressing, except the coriander and basil leaves, in a glass bowl. Cut the squid into pieces. Boil the water with the salt, put the squid pieces into the boiling water and leave them to cook, with the water just bubbling a little, for 3–4 minutes. Drain immediately.

While the squid pieces are still warm, put them into the bowl with the dressing and mix well. Let the squid cool before mixing the coriander, basil and cucumber into the salad. Adjust the seasoning with more salt if necessary. Serve at room temperature.

Anton Mosimann

Rendez-vous de Fruits-de-Mer à la Crème de Basilic

Seafood in Basil Sauce

(Cuisine à la Carte)

The very title of this dish takes me back to the heady days of *nouvelle cuisine*, when plates were big, helpings small and the cookery world full of fancy. Inevitably we make fun of *nouvelle cuisine*, its absurdities and pomposity, yet it did change cooking in significant ways. Sauces became lighter, techniques less heavy-handed, flavours more daring. The young Anton Mosimann, newly arrived from Switzerland to the kitchens of the Dorchester Hotel in London, was at the forefront of introducing this new cooking to Britain. I was then a greenhorn journalist at *Harper's & Queen* and my first encounter with Anton's original, almost lapidary cooking was both startling and stimulating. His first cookbook, *Cuisine à la Carte*, from which this recipe is taken, is aimed at professional chefs and is full of first-rate recipes and useful kitchen lore. This old standby in my kitchen is a refresh-ing way of dealing with the vicissitudes of the fishmonger's slab. As Anton says, 'A rendez-vous offers a lot of scope – one is not obliged to serve coquilles St Jacques, lobster or sole but rather whatever comes completely fresh from the market.' He presents it as a first course; I make at least twice as much and serve it as a main course with noodles or a mixture of wild and basmati rice.

Opening oysters is a tricky business – I recommend that you get your fishmonger to do it. Apart from that, the recipe is quite straight-forward for the home cook until you come to the instruction to 'monté' the sauce with butter. This is a chef's term and means that you whisk in small pieces of chilled butter a little at a time to enrich the sauce and give it a glossy appearance.

Serves 4

4 large scallops in their shells, 120g/4¹/₂oz
   net
8 scampi, removed from their shells
150g/5oz salmon, cut into 15g/¹/₂oz pieces
   lengthwise
150g/5oz turbot, cut into 15g/¹/₂oz pieces
   lengthwise
4 oysters, in their shells
20g/³/₄oz carrot, cut into thin strips
20g/³/₄oz leek, cut into thin strips

20g/³/₄oz celery, cut into thin strips
20g/³/₄oz butter
175ml/6fl oz fish stock
175ml/6fl oz dry white wine
450ml/³/₄ pint double cream
40ml/1¹/₂fl oz Noilly Prat
12 basil leaves, cut into strips
65g/2¹/₂oz butter, to finish
salt, freshly ground pepper
cayenne

Open the scallops with a small strong knife and place on the hotplate for a few minutes
to open them completely. Remove the scallops and roe with a soup spoon. Separate the
scallops carefully from the roe and wash thoroughly.

Cut the scallops in half and lay on a cloth to dry.
Season the scampi and pieces of salmon and turbot.
Open the oysters, take out the flesh and remove the beards (keep the oysters in their
   own water).
Sweat the carrot, leek and celery in the butter.
Add the turbot and scampi and continue to sweat.
Add the salmon and scallops.
Add the fish stock and white wine, bring to the boil and allow to simmer for 2 minutes.
Remove the seafood and vegetables and keep warm.
Reduce the stock, add the cream and Noilly Prat and allow to reduce a little.
Return the seafood and vegetables to the sauce.
Add the raw oysters and their water and the basil to the sauce.
Monté with butter and season to taste with salt and pepper and cayenne.
Arrange in small porcelain cocottes and serve immediately.

Note
Different seafood may be used, depending upon the season.

Mussels with Saffron

(Cooking in Ten Minutes)

No cookery writer has ever got to the point quicker than Edouard de Pomiane. This witty and delicious recipe mixes what used to be the most expensive spice in the world with the cheapest seafood you can buy. I like mussels but rarely bother cooking them because the preparation seems such a bore. In fact it's not really that much work. First wash the mussels and pull their beards off. Throw out any open ones that don't close when you tap them on the work surface. Then put them in a large pan with a little splash of white wine and some chopped shallots. Cover the pan, turn on the heat, shake the pan every now and again and in 5 minutes the mussels will be cooked. All the shells should be open. If any stay closed, chuck them out. Crush some saffron between your fingers and add to the liquid along with a knob of butter. Don't add flour as de Pomiane suggests; nowadays we like our sauces a bit thinner and all that double cream will give it just the right consistency. This can be a first course or you can make it more substantial by serving it up with some plain boiled basmati rice.

Cook two pounds [*900g*] of mussels. Put them on one side. Warm their water with an ounce [*25g*] of butter and a little saffron. Thicken with 100 grammes [*4oz*] of thick cream mixed with a teaspoonful of flour. Serve the mussels with the sauce separately in a sauceboat. This is a feast.

Maine Crabmeat Turnovers

(Jasper White's Cooking from New England)

I was born in Boston and can tell you that historically Boston was not a great restaurant city, partly because serious dining was done behind closed doors in clubs and also thanks to the New England horror of ostentation. But there's always been a strong tradition of home cooking, based on the once-abundant supply of some of the world's best seafood. Jasper White was one of the New Wave chefs who created a dynamic eating-out scene in Boston in the eighties. He now works as the top chef for Legal Seafood, a large chain of outstanding fish restaurants so called because it was started by lawyers.

You will not be able to buy fresh Maine crabmeat in Britain, which is a pity, but there is excellent crab available from Cornwall. I can't understand why crab is so undervalued. I am passionate about lobster but in truth I must admit that a good crab is no less tasty or exciting.

These turnovers make a glamorous cocktail snack, a nice lunch or a stellar first course for a grown-up dinner. White suggests serving them in the spring with a salad of fresh asparagus with a light mustard dressing. You could also serve a small green salad dressed with a little oil and sherry vinegar alongside them.

Makes 32 small turnovers

8 sheets filo pastry, 12 x 17 inches [*30 x 42cm*]

8 tablespoons [*100g/4oz*] unsalted butter, melted

For the crabmeat filling:

2 tablespoons finely diced red pepper

2 tablespoons finely diced carrot

2 tablespoons finely diced celery

1 small chilli pepper (optional)

1 tablespoon [*15g/¹/₂oz*] unsalted butter

1 pound [*450g*] fresh Maine crabmeat, drained

2 scallions [*spring onions*], finely chopped

1 tablespoon Dijon mustard

1 tablespoon mayonnaise

¹/₄ cup [*25g/1oz*] dry white breadcrumbs

juice of ¹/₂ lemon

salt and freshly ground black pepper

Sauté the pepper, carrot, celery and chilli pepper, if using, in the butter. Allow to cool, then chill. Mix with crabmeat, scallions, mustard, mayonnaise, breadcrumbs and lemon juice. Season to taste with salt and pepper. Try to mix gently so that the crabmeat is not completely shredded.

If you work fast you will not need to bother with the damp cloth that is sometimes recommended when working with filo pastry. Brush each sheet generously with the melted butter. Cut lengthwise into 4 even strips (2 inches [*5cm*] wide). Put a heaped teaspoonful of the filling in the bottom corner of a strip and fold over into a triangle. Continue folding until you reach the end of the strip. Place on a baking sheet and brush with butter. Continue until all the turnovers are done.

About 25 minutes before serving, preheat the oven to 180°C/350°F/Gas Mark 4. Bake for 12 to 15 minutes or until very crisp and golden brown.

Desserts

Patricia Lousada

Pecan Pie

(The Cooking of the USA)

A former ballet dancer from New York, Patricia Lousada is well placed to introduce real American cooking to the British public. Just as pumpkin pie is related to the English custard pie, so pecan pie is a cousin to treacle tart. (The Canadians have added another cousin to the family tree with *tarte d'érables*, which is made with maple syrup.) As much as I like treacle tart I think pecan pie is a decided improvement. The pecans give the smooth, sticky filling added interest with their crunchy texture and slightly bitter taste. In America this pie is made with something called Karo syrup, which you may be able to find through some specialist American food importers; otherwise stay (I am tempted to say 'stick') with Patricia Lousada's suggestion of dark golden syrup. You can serve this with cream, but it is best served the American way with vanilla ice cream.

Serves 8

For the pastry:
ingredients as in Pumpkin Pie pastry (see page 180)

For the filling:
3 eggs
225g/8oz soft dark brown sugar
1 teaspoon vanilla extract
¼ teaspoon salt
75g/3oz butter, melted
6 tablespoons dark golden syrup (or half light golden syrup and half black treacle)
225g/8oz shelled pecan nuts, chopped coarsely, plus a few halved to decorate

Make the pastry and form a pie shell as for Pumpkin Pie, and bake blind in an oven preheated to 200°C/400°F/Gas Mark 6. Turn the oven down to 180°C/350°F/Gas Mark 4. Lightly beat the eggs in a medium-size bowl. Beat in the sugar, vanilla extract and salt. Stir in the melted butter, syrup and chopped nuts. Pour into the partially baked pie shell and decorate with the pecan halves.

Bake in the middle of the oven on a hot baking sheet for 35–40 minutes or until the filling is set. Cover with foil if the pastry becomes too dark. Serve warm or cool with ice cream or cream.

Patricia Lousada

Pumpkin Pie

(The Cooking of the USA)

The pumpkin is just another of the many native American foods that have flourished in Europe. Europeans think of pumpkin as a savoury: Italians stuff ravioli with it and some French are partial to pumpkin soup. So serving it as a pudding seems decidedly odd. It may help you to think of it, as Patricia Lousada does, as 'related to the English custard pie'.

The mixing of English and native American culture is older than many people think. One morning shortly after the Pilgrims established their first precarious settlement at Plymouth, Massachusetts, in 1620, they were startled to see a young Indian brave walking down their village high street. As they raced for their weapons they were even more startled to hear him address them with the words, 'Welcome, Englishmen', which he had learned during some months spent in the company of visiting English fishermen farther up the coast. The Indian, Samoset, helped the Pilgrims to learn the ways of North American agriculture, thus ensuring their survival and the first Thanksgiving.

Pumpkin pie is one of the set pieces of any Thanksgiving meal but it is also eaten throughout the autumn and winter in New England, usually topped with a generous blob of whipped cream. Patricia Lousada's recipe goes right back to first principles – not quite 'first catch your pumpkin' – scooping the flesh out of a pumpkin. Most American cooks would use tinned pumpkin flesh instead, which you can buy in some food shops in the UK.

Serves 8

For the pastry:

175g/6oz flour
1/2 teaspoon salt
1 tablespoon sugar
1 teaspoon baking powder
75g/3oz unsalted butter, very cold
1 egg yolk
3–4 tablespoons double cream

For the filling:

450g/1lb pumpkin pulp (using about
   900g/2lb pumpkin)
2 large or 3 small eggs
75g/3oz soft brown sugar
4 tablespoons golden syrup
250ml/8fl oz whipping or double cream
1 1/2 teaspoons ground cinnamon
1 teaspoon ground ginger
1/4 teaspoon ground cloves
1/2 teaspoon salt

To make the pastry, sift the flour, salt, sugar and baking powder into a mixing bowl. Cut the butter into small pieces and rub into the mixture with the tips of your fingers until the mixture acquires the texture of oatmeal. Blend the egg yolk and cream together and, using a fork, stir into the flour mixture. Turn the dough out on to a lightly floured surface and knead for 10 seconds with the heel of your hand to blend. Wrap the dough in cling-film and refrigerate for at least 30 minutes.

Roll out the dough when ready and line a 24–25cm/9 1/2–10 inch pie plate. Prick the base with a fork and fill the centre with a piece of crumpled greaseproof paper weighed down with dried beans or rice. Refrigerate for 15 minutes before baking blind in an oven preheated to 200°C/400°F/Gas Mark 6 for 15 minutes. Remove the paper and beans for the last 5 minutes of the cooking time. Place on a rack to cool. Reduce the oven temperature to 190°C/375°F/Gas Mark 5.

To make the pumpkin pulp, scrape out the seeds and stringy centre from the piece of pumpkin and bake in an oven preheated to 180°C/350°F/Gas Mark 4 for about 45 minutes, until the pumpkin is tender when pierced with a fork. Scrape the pulp from the skin and reserve. Alternatively, you can cut the peeled pumpkin flesh into pieces and cook them in a small amount of water until tender, then mash.

Combine all the filling ingredients and mix together until just blended. Pour into the pie case and return to the oven for 40 minutes, or until the filling has set. If you place the pie plate on a hot baking sheet in the oven while it cooks it helps keep the bottom pastry crisp. Serve at room temperature, with cream if desired.

Patricia Wells

Tarte Tatin aux Poires

(Bistro Cooking)

Patricia Wells has had a remarkable career as an observer of the French culinary scene for the *International Herald Tribune*, as a recorder of not only the most cutting-edge cuisine (she has collaborated with Joel Robuchon) but also the vernacular (this recipe comes from her book *Bistro Cooking*) and as a writer of guidebooks – I wouldn't visit Paris without my copy of her *Food Lover's Guide to Paris*. Tarte Tatin, the famous caramelized upsidedown apple tart, has become such a favourite pudding that it's hard to believe that it was invented only this century,

by the Tatin sisters, who lived in the village of Lamotte-Beuvron near Orléans in France. Patricia Wells's version uses pears instead of apples and I must admit that I prefer it this way. If you can't buy Bosc or Anjou pears use Packham's or Comice instead and do try to buy slightly underripe ones. Patricia Wells suggests serving the warm tart with a blob of crème fraîche, which of course is good, but you could also use vanilla ice cream or whipped cream spiked with a little Poire William eau-de-vie.

Serves 8–10

6 tablespoons [*75g/3oz*] unsalted butter

7 to 8 firm pears (about 2³/₄ pounds [*1.25kg*], preferably Bosc or Anjou, peeled, quartered, and cored

¹/₂ cup [*100g/4oz*] sugar

1 recipe *Pâte Brisée* (see below)

1 cup [*250ml/8fl oz*] crème fraîche or soured

Preheat the oven to 425°F [*220°C/Gas Mark 7*].

Melt the butter in a deep 12 inch [*30cm*] skillet [*frying pan*] over medium-high heat. Stir in the pears and sugar. Cook, stirring carefully from time to time so the pears and sugar do not stick, 20 minutes. Increase the heat to high and cook until the pears and sugar are a deep, golden brown, about 15 more minutes. (If you are like me, the urge will be to stop the cooking a bit soon, so it doesn't burn. But the tart will be much prettier and taste better if you take the time to allow the pears to turn a true golden brown.) Shake the pan from time to time, and watch carefully to be sure that the pears and sugar do not burn. (If you do not have a pan large enough to cook all of the pears, cook them in 2 smaller pans, dividing the ingredients in half.)

Literally pile the pears into an unbuttered round 10¹/₂ inch [*26cm*] clear glass baking dish or a special tin-lined copper tarte Tatin pan.

Roll out the *pâte brisée* slightly larger than the dish. Place the pastry on top of the pears, tucking a bit of the dough around the edges and down into the dish. You do not need to prick the dough.

Place the tart in the centre of the oven and bake until the pears bubble and the pastry is a deep, golden brown, 35 to 40 minutes.

Remove the tart from the oven and immediately place a large, flat heatproof serving platter top-side down on top of the baking dish or pan. Invert the pan and give the bottom a firm tap, to release any pears that may be sticking to the bottom. Slowly release the baking dish, so the tart falls evenly on to the serving platter. Serve warm or at room temperature, passing a bowl of rich crème fraîche to spoon over the tart.

Pâte Brisée

1 to 1¼ cups [100–175g/4–6oz] all-purpose [*plain*] flour (do not use unbleached)
7 tablespoons [90g/3½oz] unsalted butter, chilled and cut into pieces

⅛ teaspoon salt
3 tablespoons iced water

Place 1 cup [100g/4oz] of flour, the butter and salt in a food processor. Process just until the mixture resembles coarse crumbs, about 10 seconds. Add the iced water and pulse just until the pastry begins to hold together, about 6 to 8 times. Do not let it form a ball. Transfer the pastry to waxed paper; flatten the dough into a disc. If the dough seems too sticky, sprinkle it with additional flour, incorporating 1 tablespoon at a time. Wrap the pastry in waxed paper. Refrigerate for at least 1 hour.

Jimella Lucas and Nanci Main

Swedish Cream

(The Ark Restaurant Cookbook)

The states of Oregon and Washington on the Northwest coast of America are becoming gastronomic hotspots. Inevitably, I suppose, because they have attracted refugees from food-obsessed California and also because a lot of money is being pumped into 'good living' by all the high-tech millionaires created by Northwest-based companies such as Microsoft. The Ark Restaurant on the Washington coast has been influential in developing a style of cooking based on great Northwestern produce. Jimella Lucas and Nanci Main are especially keen on desserts using berries – something we can appreciate in Britain. This pudding, which they describe as a 'sour cream custard', looks nicely old-fashioned presented in parfait glasses. Amongst their recommended toppings is a mixture of blackberries, lemon zest and amaretto liqueur or Grand Marnier. Fresh raspberries work just as well.

Serves 6

gelatine	**plain yoghurt**
water	**soured cream**
heavy [*double*] cream	**vanilla**
sugar	**Grand Marnier**

Soften 2 teaspoons gelatine in 1 tablespoon cold water in saucepan. When soft, add 1¹/₂ cups [*350ml/12fl oz*] heavy [*double*] cream, ¹/₂ cup [*100g/4oz*] sugar. Put pan on medium heat, stirring constantly with spoon until gelatine dissolves; make sure you reach to pan's corners. Do not allow mixture to boil. Remove from heat and transfer to bowl.

Let cool – about 20 minutes – stirring occasionally. Fold in ¹/₄ cup [*4 tablespoons*] plain yoghurt, ³/₄ cup [*175ml/6fl oz*] soured cream, ¹/₂ teaspoon vanilla (Mexican, if possible), 2 tablespoons Grand Marnier.

Pour into 6 serving glasses or parfait glasses; cover with plastic wrap [*clingfilm*] and refrigerate for about an hour.

Simon Hopkinson with Lindsey Bareham

Bread and Butter Pudding

(Roast Chicken and Other Stories)

It was Anton Mosimann during his time at the Dorchester who brought forth bread and butter pudding from the domestic kitchen to the restaurant table, and begat many versions in his wake. You can now find recipes for chocolate bread and butter pudding or bread and butter pudding made with baguette, panettone (wonderful) or even malt loaf. Simon uses tea cakes, taking advantage of the fact that 'the fruit and some spice is already there'. If you wanted you could add a bit more fruit and spice by chucking in some finely chopped glacé ginger or lemon zest. I greatly enjoy the Famous Five-style dénouement of this recipe, where we are advised to dish it up with 'lashings of thick cream'.

Serves 4

4 tea cakes, split and cut into half moons
100g/4oz butter, softened
2 whole eggs
3 egg yolks
250ml/8fl oz milk

150ml/¼ pint double cream
50g/2oz caster sugar
1 measure of dark rum
a pinch of salt
a little extra caster sugar

Preheat the oven to 180°C/350°F/Gas Mark 4. Lightly butter a deep oval porcelain dish. Spread the tea cakes with the butter and lay them in the dish slightly overlapping each other. Mix together the eggs, egg yolks, milk, cream and caster sugar. Stir in the rum and salt. Carefully pour over the tea cakes and leave for 30 minutes or more for the bread to soak up the custard. Lightly sprinkle with the extra sugar and bake in the oven for 30–40 minutes or until just set and golden brown. Serve warm rather than hot, with lashings of thick cream.

Flan

(Sunset Magazine)

Flan sounds so dreadful I wish it were called something else. Spain and Portugal have a well-established tradition of rich flans and pastries which seem powerfully sweet even to sugar-loving Anglo-Saxons. Similar desserts can be found throughout the countries that were part of the old Spanish and Portuguese empires – a not inconsiderable area, as you will remember from your school history classes: just over 500 years ago Pope Nicholas II divided the world up between the Spanish and the Portuguese. This flan, or caramel custard, has benefited from going native. Its smooth, eggy blandness has been transformed by a heavy infusion of colonial flavours to make a terrific concoction that is both soothingly suave and refreshingly spicy.

Serves 6–8

4 whole cloves

2 *each* whole allspice and cardamom pods, crushed

1 cinnamon stick (about 3 inches [*7.5cm*] long), broken in half

2 cups [*500ml/17fl oz*] milk

1 teaspoon vanilla

1 tablespoon cold water

²/₃ cup [*150g/5oz*] sugar

6 eggs

In a cheesecloth bag or tea ball, combine cloves, allspice, cardamom and cinnamon. Place in a pan with milk and vanilla; set aside.

In a small, heavy pan, mix water and ¹/₃ cup [*65g/2¹/₂oz*] of the sugar. Stir gently until sugar dissolves. Place pan over high heat and cook syrup, swirling pan occasionally, until clear and medium-amber in colour.

Immediately pour caramel into a 1¹/₂ quart [*1.5 litre/2¹/₂ pint*] soufflé dish or 9 inch [*23cm*] pie pan; tilt and swirl dish to evenly coat bottom and half-way up sides. Set on a wire rack to cool (caramel will harden quickly).

Heat milk and spices over medium heat until steaming hot; remove from heat and let cool slightly. Discard spices. In a large bowl, beat eggs with remaining sugar; gradually add milk, blending quickly with a wire whisk or fork. Pour egg mixture into prepared dish.

Place dish in a larger baking pan at least 2 inches [*5cm*] deep. Place on middle rack of a 350°F [*180°C/Gas Mark 4*] oven and add enough boiling water to larger pan to come half way up sides of flan dish.

Bake, uncovered, until a very shallow crevice forms when centre of custard is pushed with back of a spoon (about 25 minutes; about 15 minutes if using pie pan). Remove dish from hot water. Cover and refrigerate for at least 6 hours or until next day.

To unmould, loosen edge of flan with a knife; then cover dish with a rimmed plate. Invert quickly. (If necessary, briefly dip bottom of flan dish in hot water to loosen.) To serve, cut into wedges and top with caramel sauce.

Caroline Conran

Light Christmas Pudding

(Delicious Home Cooking)

Christmas is the greatest of all English feasts, distinguished not only by the superabundance of food and drink on offer but also by a number of unusual ritualistic dishes that reflect the unique nature of the day. Christmas pudding must be chief amongst the Christmas signifiers on the English table. Nowadays few people take the trouble to make their own: it used to be a ritual in every family. How many people remember 'Stir-up Sunday' six weeks before Christmas and so named after the collect beginning 'Stir up, we beseech thee O Lord, the wills of thy faithful people . . .', but also a useful date for stirring the Christmas pudding? This 'light' pudding does not need maturing and can be made the day before Christmas if you like. I think it might more candidly be called lighter rather than light – it's still full of the dense, complex, spicy richness that we demand from the best Christmas puddings. Caroline Conran (ex-wife of restaurateur and food mogul Sir Terence Conran) has roamed far as a cookbook writer, helping to introduce the cuisine of French chef Roger Vergé to Britain as well as interpreting the glories of Fanny Farmer's Boston cooking. In *Delicious Home Cooking* she concentrates on giving new life to many old favourites of the English kitchen, like this Christmas pudding. Any leftovers are splendid crumbled up and mixed into vanilla ice cream.

Serves 6–8

50g/2oz whole pieces of mixed candied peel

75g/3oz fine fresh wholemeal bread without crusts

225g/8oz large seedless raisins

225g/8oz sultanas

75g/3oz ground almonds

100g/4oz golden Demerara sugar

a pinch of sea salt

75g/3oz unsalted butter, softened

juice and grated rind of $1/2$ large or 1 small lemon

2 eggs

3 tablespoons brandy

1 tablespoon milk

$1/4$ teaspoon freshly grated nutmeg

$1/2$ teaspoon ground cinnamon

$1/2$ teaspoon ground mixed spice

Pour boiling water over the candied peels and let them soak for 3–4 minutes, then drain and cut into slivers. Make fine breadcrumbs with the wholemeal bread. Mix together the raisins, separated from each other with your fingers if necessary, sultanas, candied peels, ground almonds, breadcrumbs, Demerara sugar and salt. Stir or rub the butter into the dry ingredients with your fingertips, until it is well mixed in. Add the grated lemon rind and juice.

Whisk together the eggs, brandy and milk, whisking them well, then add them to the bowl and mix in. Lastly, add the spices, using less or more according to your own taste. Let everyone stir the pudding for good luck, then put the mixture into a buttered 1 litre/1$3/4$ pint pudding basin. Push in silver charms or a silver sixpence.

Place a disc of buttered greaseproof paper on top of the mixture, cover the basin loosely with a round of kitchen foil and tie it on with a piece of string, making a handle across the top to lift the pudding. Steam in a large, covered pan of boiling water for 4 hours. Top up as necessary with boiling water.

To serve: on Christmas Day itself, steam the pudding for 1 hour and serve with brandy sauce. Don't forget to pour heated brandy over the top and set it alight as the pudding makes its grand entrance at the Christmas table.

Stephanie Alexander

Sticky Toffee Pudding

(The Cook's Companion)

Gastronomic hot spots come and go: Sydney is now a major destination in every food lover's itinerary. Unsurprisingly, I suppose, since the new generation of Australian chefs is unfettered by historical and social hang-ups as well as being blessed with a dazzling market basket stuffed full of New and Old World produce. Since 1976 Stephanie Alexander has been arousing palates in once gastronomically staid Melbourne at her restaurant, Stephanie's. Her fifth book, *The Cook's Companion*, is a work with international resonance, an encyclopaedic romp through ingredients from anchovies to zucchini, full of good kitchen sense and dazzling tastes. It has very quickly become one of the most-used books in my kitchen, thanks to an Australian jaunt made by my producer on 'Masterchef', Richard Bryan. Sticky Toffee Pudding is one of Stephanie Alexander's more old-fashioned recipes, a clear and simple version of a nursery pudding that has become so popular in Britain that you can even buy it ready-made in supermarkets now. Stephanie Alexander's introduction to this recipe is short and sharp: 'This pudding has everything going for it: it is delicious, easy to make, requires no fancy equipment and everyone loves it.'

Serves 8

175g/6oz dates, stoned and chopped
1 teaspoon bicarbonate of soda
300ml/¹/₂ pint boiling water
50g/2oz butter
175g/6oz caster sugar
2 eggs
175g/6oz self-raising flour

¹/₂ teaspoon pure vanilla
For the sauce:
400g/14oz brown sugar
250ml/8fl oz thick cream
250g/9oz butter
1 vanilla pod, split

Preheat oven to 180°C/350°F/Gas Mark 4 and butter an 18cm/7 inch square cake tin. Mix dates and bicarbonate of soda. Pour over water and leave to stand.

Cream butter and sugar, then add eggs, one at a time, beating well after each. Fold flour in gently, then stir in date mixture and vanilla and pour into prepared tin. Bake in centre of oven for 30–40 minutes until cooked when tested with a skewer.

To make the sauce, bring all ingredients to a boil. Reduce heat and simmer for 5 minutes. Remove vanilla pod. Pour a little sauce over warm pudding and return it to oven for 2–3 minutes so sauce soaks in. Cut pudding into squares and pass extra sauce.

Ruth Rogers and Rose Gray
Chocolate Nemesis
(The River Café Cook Book)

Ruth Rogers and Rose Gray describe this simply as 'the best chocolate cake ever', which may explain why so many denizens of their highly fashionable restaurant are both *bella figura* and well upholstered. The goddess Nemesis was one of the most terrifying figures of Greek mythology, like a vengeful headmistress happiest when doling out punishment to those who were too proud, too smug, too darned clever or, in this case, too thin. I agree that it is 'the best chocolate cake ever' and am also reminded of a remark the late restaurateur Bob Payton made about one pudding, when he said that you might as well rub it on your hips because that was where it was going.

Some people find this recipe tricky to get right at home but I have discovered that if you halve the quantities and use a 20cm/8 inch tin (but keep to the original timings) it is extremely successful. And when you get to the syrup-making stage I'd advise you to boil the mixture for 3 to 5 minutes just to make sure it's syrupy.

Serves 10–12

10 whole eggs
600g/1lb 5oz caster sugar

675g/1¹/₂lb bitter-sweet chocolate, broken into small pieces
450g/1lb unsalted butter, softened

Preheat the oven to 160°C/325°F/Gas Mark 3. Line a 20 x 5cm (12 x 2 inch) cake tin with greaseproof paper, then grease and flour it.

Beat the eggs with a third of the sugar until the volume quadruples – this will take at least 10 minutes in an electric mixer.

Heat the remaining sugar in a small pan with 250ml/8fl oz water until the sugar has completely dissolved to a syrup.

Place the chocolate and butter in the hot syrup and stir to combine. Remove from the heat and allow to cool slightly.

Add the warm syrup to the eggs and continue to beat, rather more gently, until completely combined – about 20 seconds, no more. Pour into the cake tin and place in a bain-marie of hot water. It is essential, if the cake is to cook evenly, that the water comes up to the rim of the tin. Bake in the oven for 30 minutes or until set. Test by placing the flat of your hand gently on the surface.

Leave to cool in the tin before turning out.

Gelato di Cappuccino and Gelato di Panna
Cappuccino Ice Cream and Cream Ice Cream

(Marcella's Kitchen)

In the introduction to her majestic chapter on ice cream making in *Marcella's Kitchen*, Marcella Hazan explains how Italian ice cream manages to be so rich and velvety in texture and yet so refreshing at the same time. She tells us that Italian ice cream vendors had to sell their wares cheaply and 'ignored such expensive ingredients as cream and butter. Their necessity was our good fortune. To attain lightness, ice cream must absorb air and swell as it is beaten in the freezing machine. Heavy fats hamper this process. When made by home methods, very rich ice cream is ponderous.' Extra cream does not a better ice cream make; the secret is more vigorous and thorough churning. This is the time to use your ice cream machine.

The cappuccino ice cream is sharp and bracing, an ideal pick-me-up after an elaborate dinner. Marcella Hazan comments that she prefers it made this way with very little sugar, but you might wish to add a little more. Be aware that this recipe contains uncooked egg yolks if you are nervous about such things. The cream ice cream is less austere than Marcella Hazan's other ice cream recipes and uses double cream for flavouring as well as richness. This is as close to elemental ice cream as you can get, indescribably good with chocolate sauce or maple syrup, with a warm apple tart or on its own. Although Marcella Hazan suggests it serves 6–8, I reckon it provides 4 decent helpings.

Gelato di Cappuccino
Cappuccino Ice Cream

Serves 4

600ml/1 pint milk

8 tablespoons espresso coffee grounds,
 regular grind

2 small egg yolks

50g/2oz granulated sugar

Put the milk and coffee grounds in a saucepan and turn the heat to medium. When the milk comes to a boil, let it bubble for 5 minutes, stirring steadily.

Line a strainer with 4 layers of cheesecloth and set it over a bowl. Pour the milk and coffee solution into the strainer. It will drip very slowly, separating the liquid from the grounds. When the rate at which it drips becomes very intermittent, help the liquid through the cheesecloth by stirring it with a spoon. At the end, pick up the ends of the cloth and twist, applying gentle pressure, to force through as much of the remaining liquid as possible.

Beat the 2 egg yolks together with the sugar until they form pale, foamy ribbons.

Pour the milk and coffee solution into the beaten egg yolks in a slow, thin stream, beating constantly with a whisk or fork. If at the end you see a deposit of coffee grounds, stop pouring.

Set aside to cool completely, then freeze in an ice cream machine, following the manufacturer's instructions.

Gelato di Panna
Cream Ice Cream

Serves 6–8

250ml/8fl oz milk

250ml/8fl oz double cream

4 tablespoons granulated sugar

Put all the ingredients in a small saucepan, turn the heat to medium, and bring to a low, controlled boil.

Cook, stirring constantly, for 10 minutes.

Transfer to a bowl and allow to cool completely.

Place in an ice cream maker and freeze according to the manufacturer's instructions.

Ben Cohen and Jerry Greenfield

Jerry's Chocolate Ice Cream

(Ben & Jerry's Homemade Ice Cream and Desserts Book)

There are two great mass-produced ice creams: Häagen-Dazs and Ben & Jerry's. While they have different images and a different range of flavours, what they share is the American style of a rich, thick-enough-to-chew, full-of-bits ice cream. I like them both, but have often worried that their success has probably driven many small-town artisan ice cream makers out of business. I spent a day in upstate Vermont – a state with more cows than people – visiting Ben and was absolutely convinced of his zeal for ice cream (which as a New Englander I share) and passion for quality. This chocolate ice cream uses the old cook's trick of adding cocoa powder to chocolate for an even more chocolatey taste as well as what Jerry describes as a more complex 'mouthfeel'. You won't be able to get unsweetened chocolate in the UK so go for a high-quality dark chocolate with 70 per cent cocoa solids instead. If you don't have an ice cream maker, you can still make this, as long as you beat it periodically as it is freezing. I find that after about a week in the freezer homemade ice cream begins to go a bit stale, so eat it up.

Makes about 900ml/1½ pints

2 ounces [*50g*] unsweetened chocolate
⅓ cup [*40g/1½oz*] unsweetened cocoa
** powder**
1½ cups [*350ml/12fl oz*] milk
2 large eggs

1 cup [*225g/8oz*] sugar
1 cup [*250ml/8fl oz*] heavy [*double*] or
** whipping cream**
1 teaspoon vanilla extract

Melt the unsweetened chocolate in the top of a double boiler over hot, not boiling, water. Gradually whisk in the cocoa and heat, stirring constantly, until smooth. (The chocolate may 'seize' or clump together. Don't worry, the milk will dissolve it.) Whisk in the milk, a little at a time, and heat until completely blended. Remove from the heat and let cool.

Whisk the eggs in a mixing bowl until light and fluffy, 1 to 2 minutes. Whisk in the sugar, a little at a time, then continue whisking until completely blended, about 1 minute more. Pour in the cream and vanilla and whisk to blend.

Pour the chocolate mixture into the cream mixture and blend. Cover and refrigerate until cold, about 1 to 3 hours, depending on your refrigerator.

Transfer the mixture to an ice cream maker and freeze following the manufacturer's instructions.

Variation: Chocolate Chocolate Chip
Add ¾ cup [*75g/3oz*] semisweet chocolate chips after the ice cream stiffens (about 2 minutes before it is done), then continue freezing until the ice cream is ready.

Anna del Conte

Spumone di Zabaglione
Zabaglione Ice Cream

(Secrets from an Italian Kitchen)

I love making ice cream. Or perhaps I should say that I love the idea of making ice cream. Like a lot of other people, I bought a very powerful, impressive and easy-to-use ice cream machine which spends a lot of time resting in the back of an infrequently opened kitchen cupboard. This recipe is a good excuse for dusting the old machine off and giving it a whirl. However, you can also make it by hand because the recipe for the base features enough alcohol and sugar to keep the mixture creamy. But you still have to give it a whisk as it freezes, otherwise you get the bane of all decent ice cream — ice crystals.

For my taste this is far better than ordinary zabaglione, which I find both cloying and insubstantial. For a major experience, try serving it with sliced Italian white peaches.

Serves 6

5 eggs
100g/4oz caster sugar
pinch of ground cinnamon
120ml/4fl oz Marsala

2 tablespoons rum
300ml/½ pint double cream
amarettini or chopped hazelnuts

Separate the eggs and put the yolks in a bowl or in the top of a double boiler. Put 3 of the whites in another bowl.

Add the sugar and the cinnamon to the egg yolks and beat off the heat until the custard becomes pale yellow and forms ribbons. Add the Marsala and the rum, while beating constantly. Put the bowl over a saucepan one-third full of hot water, or on to the bottom half of the double saucepan. Bring the water to the simmer while you whisk constantly – an electric beater is ideal for the job. The mixture will become foamy and will nearly double in volume. Put the bowl in cold water and leave it to cool, beating very frequently.

Whip the cream until it forms soft peaks, then incorporate the egg custard into the cream.

Whip the 3 egg whites until they form stiff peaks. Add the whipped egg white by the spoonful to the egg and cream mixture, folding it in gently.

If you have an ice cream machine, follow the manufacturer's instructions. If not, transfer the zabaglione mixture to a large glass dish and place in the freezer. About 3 hours later remove from the freezer and, with a metal whisk or an electric beater, beat the zabaglione. This stirring will break up any crystals that might have formed and make the mixture smooth and velvety. Return to the freezer and leave for at least 4 hours.

You can decorate the *spumone* with *amarettini* – small *amaretti* – or sprinkle chopped hazelnuts over the top.

Sheila Ferguson

Apple Brown Betty and Philadelphia Ice Cream

(Soul Food)

If you like soul music you will remember the Philly Sound – slick, lavishly orchestrated Afro-American pop which rode high in the Seventies charts. The Three Degrees were amongst its leading exponents and enjoyed a certain status in Britain for being Prince Charles's favourite group. Their lead singer, Sheila Ferguson, is an excellent and enthusiastic cook who wrote a lively and inspirational book, *Soul Food*, exploring the often neglected culinary traditions of Black America, along with numerous references to the food and cooking of her Philadelphia childhood. Apple Brown Betty is as American as apple pie, and often featured on menus when I was a child. It is similar to a

British crumble and remarkably easy to make. Like a classic American apple pie, much depends on the tartness of the filling so choose a firm apple such as a Granny Smith and don't hold back on the lemon juice. Sheila Ferguson recommends serving it with custard or cream. I would suggest a more thoroughly American approach and serve warm Apple Brown Betty with cold vanilla ice cream. Sheila's ice cream recipe is eggless and elemental and she stakes a claim for Philadelphia as the birthplace of American ice cream, writing that a French confectioner set up America's first ice cream shop there in 1794.

Apple Brown Betty

Serves 6

2 cups [100g/4oz] soft breadcrumbs
¼ teaspoon salt
¼ cup [50g/2oz] melted butter or margarine
4 cups tart sliced apples (4 medium apples)
¾ cup [175g/6oz] light brown sugar

1 teaspoon ground cinnamon
2 tablespoons fresh lemon juice
grated rind of 1 lemon
¼ cup [4 *tablespoons*] water at room
   temperature

Preheat your oven to 180°C/350°F/Gas Mark 4.

Mix the breadcrumbs with the salt and melted butter or margarine, and divide the mixture into three. Place one-third in a greased 1½ quart [*1.5 litres/2½ pint*] baking dish.

Sprinkle your apples with sugar, cinnamon, lemon juice and grated rind and toss to blend. Place one-half of this mixture on top of the crumbs in the baking dish. Add another one-third of the crumbs, then the remaining apples, and a final layer of crumbs. Trickle the water into the side of the dish so as not to moisten the top layer of crumbs.

Cover and bake in the oven for 30 minutes. Remove the cover and continue to bake until the apples are tender and the crumbs a delicious brown, perhaps another 20 or 30 minutes. Serve warm with cream or custard.

Philadelphia Ice Cream

Serves 6

4 cups [*1 litre/1¾ pints*] light [*single*] cream
   (or equal parts heavy [*double*] and light
   cream)
1 cup [225g/8oz] sugar

⅛ teaspoon salt
1½ tablespoons pure vanilla extract
   (or 1 tablespoon vanilla extract and
   1 teaspoon finely crushed vanilla pod)

In a medium saucepan over low heat, heat your cream to just lukewarm. *Do not let it boil!* Stir in the sugar, salt and vanilla until the sugar dissolves completely. Let it cool slightly, then freeze in your ice cream maker according to the manufacturer's directions.

If you don't have an ice cream machine, turn the temperature of your freezer as low as it will go and freeze the mixture in shallow metal pie pans [*pie plates*]. After 45 minutes to 1 hour, depending on the temperature, the mixture will have frozen to the consistency of thick slush. Tip it into a food processor and beat it quickly (or into a bowl and beat it hard with a fork), then return to the pans and the freezer. Repeat every 45 minutes until the ice cream has a good texture, 2 to 4 hours according to the temperature.

Brown Bread Ice Cream with Rum

(Michael Smith's New English Cookery)

The late Michael Smith was a great exponent of English cookery, and his work updating our traditional ways certainly made many cooks turn back to their native culinary roots. Sadly, he died before the high watermark of television cookery – what a great impact he would have made in broadcasting. His influence endures not just through his books (and he is one of those rare writers who makes you taste what he describes) but also thanks to the Michael Smith Prize, which the Guild of Food Writers gives out each year for the best book on British food.

The affluent amongst our Georgian ancestors were enthusiastic eaters of ice cream, and brown bread ice cream is supposedly an 18th-century dish, presumably concocted because there was so much stale bread lying around in the kitchens of great houses. Sadly, the bright spark who first came up with the eccentric idea of adding crumbs to frozen custard was most likely some anonymous kitchen servant whose name we'll never know.

Some recipes for this ice cream merely toast the crumbs under a grill. Smith goes the delicious extra step and cooks them in butter and sugar. He also recommends adding the crumbs after the ice cream begins to set, which avoids any muddy colours.

When I was growing up in New England, a local favourite – which I still love – was Grape Nut ice cream. Just follow Michael Smith's recipe, leaving out any of the steps to do with breadcrumbs, and as the ice cream thickens add 175g/6oz Grape Nuts. And yes, I do mean the breakfast cereal.

Serves 6–8

For the basic custard ice cream:

8 egg yolks

75g/3oz caster sugar

600ml/1 pint single cream

1/2 vanilla pod or 1 teaspoon vanilla extract

3 tablespoons Jamaica rum

For the brown bread:

175g/6oz good rich brown breadcrumbs

50g/2oz unsalted butter, melted

50g/2oz caster sugar

Beat the egg yolks and sugar until creamy white and fluffy in a non-stick pan. Bring the cream to boiling point with the vanilla pod (or extract). Remove the pod and pour the cream over the egg mixture, whisking briskly. Return the mixture to the pan and, over the lowest possible heat, stir all the time, covering the base of the pan meticulously, until the custard coats the back of a wooden spoon well. Pour into a bowl and leave to cool. Add the rum to the cooled custard. Churn, following the instructions on your particular machine.

Gently fry the breadcrumbs in the butter, patiently stirring them around in the pan. Sprinkle over the sugar and let this caramelize. Cool. Crush to fine crumbs with a rolling pin. Put half this mixture into the ice cream just as it is beginning to set. Serve the remainder as a crunchy topping, with a spoonful or two of thick cream as well.

Josceline Dimbleby

Orange and Cardamom Ice Cream with Orange Blossom and Walnut Syrup

(Josceline Dimbleby's Book of Puddings, Desserts and Savouries)

I unashamedly present another ice cream recipe on the assumption that you can't have too many. Ice cream has become so easy to make, especially if you have one of the better electric machines, yet it still seems like a very special treat. Josceline Dimbleby's fascination with Middle Eastern and Asian flavours has given an exotic inflection to many of her recipes. This one is worthy of any harem or grand dinner party. As she explains, 'Luxurious, creamy ice creams are always a great success, but I think this is the favourite of them all. It is aromatic, rich and creamy, yet still fresh-flavoured. The scented syrup and crunchy nuts give an exciting contrast in texture.' This recipe very much took the fancy of one of Australia's most influential chefs, Stephanie Alexander (for more about her, see page 190), and has helped make Jossy a gastro-celebrity down under. Although most people think of ice cream as a summertime dish, the flavours and perfume of this one are actually rather wintry and Christmassy.

1 can frozen concentrated orange juice

3 large eggs

1/2 teaspoon salt

175g/6oz caster sugar

6 tablespoons water

5–6 cardamom pods

300ml/1/2 pint double or whipping cream

For the syrup:

100g/4oz caster sugar

4 tablespoons water

2 tablespoons orange flower water

1 tablespoon lemon juice

25g/1oz walnuts, roughly chopped

First leave the frozen orange juice to thaw a bit. Whisk the eggs with the salt until frothy. Dissolve the sugar in the water over a low heat. Then boil fiercely without stirring for 3 minutes. Pour the bubbling syrup immediately on to the eggs, whisking all the time at high speed. Continue whisking until the mixture has thickened quite a bit. Remove the seeds from the cardamom pods, crush finely in a pestle and mortar and add to the mixture. Then whisk in the concentrated orange juice thoroughly. Lastly whip the cream until thick but not stiff and fold into the ice cream mixture. Pour into a dish or into a mould and freeze for several hours.

While the ice cream is freezing make the syrup. Dissolve the sugar in the water over a low heat, bring to the boil and boil fiercely for 1 minute. Remove from the heat and stir in the orange flower water and the lemon juice strained through a sieve. Stir in the chopped walnuts and leave to cool. Before serving the ice cream pour the syrup over the top. If you have frozen it in a mould, dip briefly in hot water, turn out on to a serving plate, then pour the syrup over just before putting it on the table.

James Beard

Strawberries Romanov, Peaches with Raspberry Purée and Drunken Watermelon

(The Theory and Practice of Good Cooking)

The late James Beard was in his lifetime the colossus of American cookery. Scholarly and pragmatic, his books are as much about a philosophy of food as they are collections of recipes. He was clever without being tricky, and the absolute master of the small details that can elevate any dish.

Fresh fruit can make the best pudding but in today's global marketplace, where everything is 'fresh' all the time, you have to buy your fruit carefully. You will almost invariably find that, in spite of the wonders of airfreight and advanced refrigeration, seasonal local produce is best. There will never be anything to equal the taste of English strawberries in June. Strawberries Romanov is a fabulous dish – Beard describes it as 'simple, but extraordinarily good' – which manages to combine the clean, clear flavours of ripe strawberries and fresh orange with a whiff of the elaborate decadence that characterized late-19th-century *haute cuisine* as codified by Escoffier. With this dish you can get away with imported strawberries, although it will only be half as good.

You will probably recognize Peaches with Raspberry Purée as an ice-creamless Pêches Melba, another great dish invented by Escoffier and one of a number (including Melba toast) named after the Australian opera singer Dame Nellie Melba. I have felt a slight kinship with Nellie ever since, at the Royal Fine Arts Commission 'Building of the Year Award', Norman St John Stevas described me as 'the most exciting personality to arrive in Britain since Dame Nellie Melba'. I'm still not quite sure what he meant.

To make raspberry purée, all you need to do is purée fresh or frozen raspberries, push them through a sieve to get rid of the seeds and then sweeten to taste if necessary.

Finally, a surprising and amusing way to serve up watermelon. Beard suggests champagne, brandy or light rum; I think light rum works best and, as always, do tell your guests when there's booze hidden in the dish.

Strawberries Romanov

Serves 4

Wash and hull 450g/1lb large, ripe strawberries. Put them into a bowl and sprinkle them with sugar, if necessary. Add 200ml/7fl oz freshly squeezed orange juice and 5 tablespoons orange-flavoured liqueur and let the strawberries macerate for 1 hour. Transfer the berries to a chilled serving dish, draining off some of the liquid. Whip 350ml/12fl oz double cream and sweeten it with 2 tablespoons sugar. Spread the cream over the berries and decorate the dish with candied violets.

Peaches with Raspberry Purée

Serves 8

Peel and halve 8 peaches and arrange them in a serving dish. Sprinkle them with 2 tablespoons sugar and 1 tablespoon lemon juice, or more to taste. Spoon raspberry purée over the peaches and serve them with single cream or kirsch-flavoured whipped cream.

Raspberry purée may also be spooned over peeled and sliced peaches. Serve with double cream or crème fraîche.

Drunken Watermelon

Cut a deep plug about 5cm/2 inches square out of the top of a ripe watermelon. Remove the plug and slowly pour in as much light rum, brandy or champagne as the melon will absorb. Replace the plug and seal with masking tape. Refrigerate the melon for 24 hours, turning it 4 or 5 times to allow the liquor or wine to seep through the pulp. Serve in slices, like ordinary watermelon.

Pistachio Crème Brûlée

(Desserts – A Lifelong Passion)

The history of sweet things is studded with as many landmarks and heroes as that of any other great science. For example, Stanislas Leszcsynski brought the baba to France from Poland in 1740; Carême invented the croquembouche in the early 19th century and raised puff pastry to new heights with the vol-au-vent. Michel Roux is part of this grand tradition, cooking with the mixture of passion and precision that is the measure of a great *pâtissier*. I find many of his recipes too demanding for me even to attempt, but I enjoy reading them because they are stuffed full of a tremendous amount of kitchen craft.

This is a wonderful crème brûlée. Note the use of half milk and half whipping cream for a creamy but not cloyingly rich texture. The custards may seem a little too wobbly for comfort after cooking. Don't worry; they'll firm up as they cool. Domestic grills aren't hot enough to give a perfectly caramelized top so now is the time to have a bit of fun with a small blowtorch. You can buy one easily at a DIY shop.

Serves 6

500ml/17fl oz milk	250g/9oz caster sugar
500ml/17fl oz whipping cream	200g/7oz egg yolks
50g/2oz pistachio paste (see Notes below)	25g/1oz skinned pistachios

The custard: heat the milk, cream, pistachio paste and 75g/3oz of the sugar in a saucepan, whisking continuously at first.

In a bowl, lightly whisk the egg yolks with 50g/2oz sugar until slightly pale. As soon as the milk comes to the boil, pour it on to the eggs, little by little, whisking all the time. Cooking the custards: preheat the oven to 100°C/200°F/Gas Mark ¼.

Ladle the custard into six 15cm/6 inch gratin dishes and cook in the warm oven for 30 minutes. Remove from the oven and carefully slide the dishes on to a wire rack. Once the custards are completely cold, transfer them to the fridge.

Presentation: just before serving, sprinkle the tops of the crèmes brûlées with 65g/2½oz sugar and caramelize them with a blowtorch, or under a very hot grill, to make a thin, pale nut-brown topping.

Heat an empty small frying pan, then toss in the pistachios, sprinkle them with the remaining sugar and stir vigorously for 1 minute so that they are well coated with the sugar. Tip them on to a plate, separate the pistachios with a fork and arrange about 8 pistachios on top of each crème brûlée. Serve immediately.

Notes

The sugar topping will soften within an hour or two, depending on the humidity, so I would recommend that you caramelize the crèmes brûlées only a short time before serving.

If you cannot buy commercially made pistachio paste, make your own by pounding freshly skinned pistachios in a small mortar to make a very smooth purée.

Raymond Blanc

Clafoutis aux Cerises

(Cooking for Friends)

Raymond Blanc began his career in England working at The Rose Revived, a pretty riverside pub in Oxfordshire that I used to visit. I got to know him when he opened his own restaurant in the Summertown neighbourhood of Oxford, just near the studios of BBC Radio Oxford where I began my broadcasting career. There are few cooks anywhere in Europe as passionate and proficient as Ray, but he has never lost touch with what you could call the fundamentals of cooking.

Clafoutis is a dish of the utmost simplicity. Raymond calls it a batter cake; I would describe it as a baked pancake. Although it is a dish of impeccable peasant ancestry, for some reason it has remained unpopular even though chefs now maniacally search for country dishes to elevate to restaurant status. Once you eat it you will make clafoutis part of your regular repertoire. Traditionally the cherries are left unstoned, with disastrous consequences for your guests' dentistry: I prefer Raymond's slightly more genteel version. You can use red cherries instead of black, or try pears, apples or fresh (not dried) apricots.

Serves 4–6

500g/1lb 2oz black cherries, stoned
4 tablespoons Kirsch (optional)
100ml/3¹/₂fl oz milk
150ml/¹/₄ pint whipping cream
¹/₂ vanilla pod, or 2 drops vanilla essence

4 eggs
120g/4¹/₂oz caster sugar
20g/³/₄oz plain flour
a pinch of salt
butter and sugar for greasing and sprinkling

Preheat the oven to 200°C/400°F/Gas Mark 6.

If using the Kirsch, sprinkle over the cherries and stir. Bring the milk, cream and vanilla to the boil. Turn off the heat and leave to infuse for a few minutes.

Place the eggs and the sugar in a mixing bowl and whisk until creamy. Add the flour and salt and whisk until smooth. Then strain in the vanilla milk, beating to amalgamate.

Generously butter a 25 x 23cm/10 x 9 inch ovenproof dish, about 5cm/2 inches high, and sprinkle with caster sugar. Add the cherries, then pour the batter mixture over the cherries.

Cook in the preheated oven for 25 minutes. Remove, allow to cool until warm, and sprinkle over some caster sugar. Serve to your guests.

Banana Tarts

(Real Cooking)

Until I discovered this recipe I thought that there were only three decent ways to eat a banana: 1) as is; 2) grilled until the skin turns black, then opened up and sprinkled with brown sugar, splashed with dark rum and topped with a blob of double cream; 3) peeled, dipped in chocolate, shoved in the freezer and then eaten like a choc ice. This recipe joins the banana pantheon. Like so many of Nigel Slater's recipes it is easy, fun to make and tastes fabulous. He specifies ready-made puff pastry – you can even use ready-rolled pastry sheets for this. It is an ideal emergency pudding: good enough for guests, but perhaps even more enjoyable as pure self-indulgence in front of the television with a glass of cold Beaumes de Venise. If you want to make it a little fancier you could refine the glaze by buying a jar of cheap apricot jam, heating it until it is runny, then straining it through a sieve. The result is a professional pastry chef's glaze and you can put the bits caught in the sieve on your toast the next morning.

This recipe also works with sliced peaches or pears, though neither of them is quite as sinful as the banana version.

Makes 4

225g/8oz chilled ready-made puff pastry
4 bananas
a little melted butter

a little caster sugar (say, 2 tablespoons)
4 tablespoons apricot jam

Roll the puff pastry out into a large square about 28cm/11 inches on each side. Using a plate or bowl as a guide, cut four 13cm/5 inch circles of pastry. Transfer them to a baking sheet and put them in the fridge for 20 minutes.

Remove the pastry. Preheat the oven to 200°C/400°F/Gas Mark 6. Peel the bananas. Slice each one into rounds about twice as thick as a pound coin. Divide the bananas between the pastry, overlapping the slices where necessary. They can be higgledy-piggledy if you like. Brush them, and the pastry edges, with a little melted butter and sprinkle with sugar. Bake in the preheated oven for about 10 minutes until the pastry has puffed up and the bananas are soft.

Spread the apricot jam over the tarts and return to the oven for a further couple of minutes until they are sticky and bubbling. Eat warm with vanilla ice cream.

Martin Webb and Richard Whittington

Quince and Polenta Crumble

(The Fusion)

This pudding has all the cuddly, nursery-food qualities of the great British crumble but with added gastronomic interest. If you have a quince tree in your garden you will be familiar with the fruit – plump, rock hard and powerfully perfumed. No quince tree means a trip to a Greek or Middle Eastern food shop, or one of our more adventurous greengrocers. The quince hardly figures in Anglo-American gastronomy, although the French, Portuguese and Spanish make nice variations of quince jelly. The drawback of this recipe is the amount of time it may take you to peel, core and chop the quinces. It

may be a good opportunity to listen to an opera you haven't heard yet: just make sure it's Wagner.

Even if you don't fancy the quince – and I think you should give it a try – the polenta crumble mix is a splendid idea. It's worth making two or three times the quantity and storing the extra in the fridge. It is particularly good as a crumble topping for apple or sliced banana. I confess to enjoying my crumble with a large dollop of vanilla ice cream but I am also partial to double cream that has had some brown sugar and cinnamon stirred into it.

Serves 6

1kg/2¼lb quinces (about 3 large ones)
100g/4oz caster sugar
juice of ½ lemon
450ml/¾ pint double cream

For the crumble:

150g/5oz unsalted butter at room temperature, diced
175g/6oz polenta
150g/5oz self-raising flour
50g/2oz caster sugar

Put the sugar and lemon juice in a pan with 300ml/½ pint of water and bring to the boil. Turn down to a simmer. Peel, quarter and core the quinces, then cut the flesh into thick slices. Add to the syrup and cook for 45 minutes. Strain through a colander, reserving the syrup, and leave to cool.

Preheat the oven to 180°C/350°F/Gas Mark 4.

Make the crumble: put the butter into a bowl and allow to soften at room temperature. When soft, rub in the other ingredients to a coarse crumb consistency, which takes about 4 minutes. It does not matter if you get some of it holding in larger lumps.

Spread the quince pieces to cover the bottom of a 25cm/10 inch long, deep-sided baking dish to a depth of about 4cm/1½ inches. Top evenly with the crumble and bake for 1 hour.

About 5 minutes before it is due to come out of the oven, warm the syrup through and put into a jug for people to help themselves, also offering double cream at the table.

Bakewell Pudding

(Traditional Dishes of Britain)

Philip Harben was the first great British television cook. His tubby, bearded man-in-a-pinney shtick flickered across the nation's black and white sets in the late Forties and Fifties. In fact he wasn't the first cook to appear on television. That honour goes to the French restaurateur Marcel X. Boulestin, who broke some eggs and made an omelette for the BBC on the eve of World War II. Harben cooked and broadcast with passion and ebullience to a Britain that frankly wasn't much interested in food. His book *Traditional Dishes of Britain* admirably records many of the classics of the British kitchen in an almost anthropologically authentic form. It is rich in anecdote and cookery lore and ought to be reprinted as a monument to Harben.

Everyone has eaten, and possibly enjoyed, Bakewell pudding, although it may have been incorrectly named Bakewell tart. It provides proof to the world that pudding is a British forte. Ground almonds are now considered essential in the filling but, as Philip Harben's recipe shows, they were not part of the original. You could use bought puff pastry rather than make your own. I like to beat the egg yolks with the butter and sugar and whisk the egg whites to stiffish peaks before folding them together as this gives a lighter result. I would recommend baking the pudding on a metal baking sheet, which will help your pudding avoid 'soggy bottom'.

Make puff paste with ½lb [*225g*] flour and ½lb [*225g*] butter. Roll it out to ¼ inch [*5mm*] thickness and with it line an oval flan ring 9 inches by 7 inches [*23 x 18cm*] (or an 8 inch [*20cm*] circular ring). Pummel the base with your thumb or prick it thoroughly, so as to break down the puff-paste structure here and prevent it from rising too much and throwing out the filling.

Melt together 2oz [*50g*] caster sugar and 2oz [*50g*] butter. Mix this with the yolks of 3 eggs and the whites of 2. This is the filling.

Spread the paste in the flan ring with strawberry jam, pour the filling over it.

Bake in a hot oven (Gas Mark 7/425°F [*220°C*]) for 15 minutes, then in a medium oven (Gas Mark 4/350°F [*180°C*]) for 25 minutes.

Serve hot or cold.

Summer Pudding

(Summer Cooking)

When I first moved to Britain I was mesmerized by two indigenous dishes: summer pudding and Scotch eggs. The Scotch egg seemed plausible – after all, there is a delicious and very similar Indian concoction called *nargessi koofta* – but tasted utterly revolting. Summer pudding – stale bread soggified with berries – sounded ridiculous, but tasted sublime. It became one of my favourite puddings, so much so that Anton Mosimann made a fabulous version for my wedding lunch.

Elizabeth David's summer pudding is commendably spartan – just raspberries and redcurrants. No blueberries, no passion fruit, no kiwis, no cherries. Just raspberries and redcurrants, but make sure that the raspberries are homegrown or as near as dammit. There are, of course, numerous variations. I remember a particularly amusing one for Funereal Summer Pudding, which used blackberries and blackcurrants. Experiment by all means. But please only use native berries and never, ever prepare a summer pudding out of season. It's such a simple dish that it requires the flavour of fresh fruit. Like Elizabeth David, I believe that summer pudding is better without cream but most people will want double cream and plenty of it.

For 4 people stew 1lb [*450g*] of raspberries and ¼lb [*100g*] of redcurrants with about ¼lb [*100g*] of sugar. No water. Cook them only 2 or 3 minutes, and leave to cool. Line a round fairly deep dish (a soufflé dish does very well) with slices of one-day-old white bread with the crust removed. The bread should be of the thickness usual for sandwiches. The dish must be completely lined, bottom and sides, with no space through which the juice can escape. Fill up with the fruit, but reserve some of the juice. Cover the fruit with a complete layer of bread. On top put a plate which fits exactly inside the dish, and on the plate put a 2 or 3lbs weight. Leave overnight in a very cold larder or refrigerator. When ready to serve turn the pudding out on to a dish (not a completely flat one, or the juice will overflow) and pour over it the reserved juice.

Thick fresh cream is usually served with Summer Pudding, but it is almost more delicious without.

Maury Rubin

Lemon Tart Four Ways

(The Book of Tarts)

There has been a revival of craftsman baking in America and I hope the same thing will happen in Britain, where many of our best old-fashioned bakers have been driven under by industrial-scale enterprises. One of the prime exponents of the new American baking is Maury Rubin of the City Bakery in Manhattan, just around the corner from one of the most popular New York restaurants, the Union Square Café. Lemon tart is such a perfect dessert, with just enough acidity to cleanse the palate and refresh the spirits after even the most turgid dinner. Maury Rubin has come up with four different ways to present his delicious, sour-sweet, creamy lemon tart: in a standard pastry case; in a chocolate pastry case; as mini-tarts; or as a dramatic lemon meringue tart. They're all good but I particularly love the combination of lemon and chocolate. I also like a large glob of this filling on a pancake or waffle for Saturday breakfast.

This recipe also works with lime: just substitute the grated zest of two limes for the zest of one lemon and freshly squeezed lime juice for the lemon juice. Do not in any circumstances ever use pre-squeezed reconstituted lemon or lime juice in this or any other worthwhile recipe.

Makes 6 tarts or 34 mini-tarts

1 cup [225g/8oz] granulated sugar
grated zest of 1 lemon (see method)
1/2 cup [120ml/4fl oz] freshly squeezed lemon juice
4 large eggs
1 large egg yolk
12 tablespoons [175g/6oz] unsalted butter, cut into 6 pieces

6 fully baked tart shells, made with Standard Tart Dough (see below) or Chocolate Tart Dough (see page 216), or 34 2¼ inch [5.5cm] mini-tart shells, made with either dough
1 ounce [25g] bittersweet chocolate, melted, for design, or cocoa powder, for dusting

Place the sugar in a medium bowl and grate the zest of the lemon into it. Rub the zest and sugar together between the palms of your hands.

Strain the lemon juice into a medium nonreactive saucepan. Add the eggs, egg yolk, butter and the zested sugar, and whisk to combine. Set the pan over medium heat and cook, whisking constantly, for 3 to 5 minutes, until the mixture begins to thicken. Be sure to whisk all over the bottom of the pan, especially the edges. At the first sign of a boil, remove from the heat and strain into a bowl.

With a ladle or a large spoon, fill the tart shells with lemon cream. Refrigerate for 30 minutes or until set. To fill mini-tart shells, transfer the lemon cream to a small glass, and pour the filling into the shells.

Fill a pastry bag with the melted chocolate, if using, and stripe and dot each tart or mini-tart to make a simple design, or dust the tops with cocoa powder. Let sit at room temperature for 10 minutes before serving.

Standard Tart Dough

13 tablespoons [190g/6½oz] unsalted butter, cut into 13 pieces
1/3 cup [35g/ 1¼oz] confectioners' sugar [icing sugar]

1 large egg yolk
1½ cups [175g/6oz] unbleached all-purpose [plain] flour
1 tablespoon heavy [double] cream

Let the butter sit at room temperature for 10 to 15 minutes. It should be malleable but still cool.

Place the confectioners' sugar in the bowl of a food mixer or a medium mixing bowl. Add the butter and toss to coat. Using the paddle attachment or a hand-held mixer, cream the sugar and butter at medium speed until the sugar is no longer visible. Scrape down the sides of the bowl. Add the egg yolk and beat until well blended. Scrape down the sides of the bowl again. Add half of the flour and beat until the dough becomes crumbly. Stop the machine, add the remaining flour and then the cream, and beat until the dough forms a sticky mass. Shape the dough into a disc and wrap well in plastic. Refrigerate until firm, approximately 2 hours.

Dust a work surface with flour. Cut the chilled dough into 1 inch [2.5cm] pieces. Using the heel of your hand, knead the pieces back together into a smooth disc. As you work, use a dough scraper to free the dough from the surface if necessary. Keeping the surface well dusted, roll the disc into a 12 inch [30cm] log. Cut into 6 pieces. Refrigerate for 5 minutes.

Dust the work surface and a rolling pin with flour. Using your fist, flatten one piece of dough into a 2 to 3 inch [5–7.5cm] round. Lift it up off the work surface to dust underneath with flour. Using the rolling pin, roll the dough into a 6 inch [15cm] round about 1/8 inch [3mm] thick. With a fork, prick holes all over the dough. If the dough is too soft to handle at this point, use a dough scraper to move it to a small baking sheet and refrigerate it for 2 to 3 minutes before proceeding.

Centre the round of dough over a 4 3/4 inch [7cm] fluted tart pan with a removable bottom. Be careful that the sharp top edge does not tear the dough. With your thumbs on the inside and the tips of your fingers outside, run your hands around the tart pan several times, easing the dough down into it. Speed does not matter, finesse does. Lower your thumbs to the inside bottom of the tart pan and press to form a clean angle without excess dough build-up. Keeping your thumbs on the inside of the tart pan, again circle around it, applying light pressure to the sides; if you move the pan around through your hands, the process will be easier. There should be at least a 1/2 inch [1.25cm] rim of excess dough extending above the top edge. Roll the rolling pin over the top to trim the excess. Repeat this process with the remaining pieces of dough. (Refrigerate the scraps from each piece as you work, then combine them and refrigerate or freeze for another use.) Place the tart pans on a baking sheet. Place in the freezer for 30 minutes.

Position a rack in the centre of the oven, and preheat the oven to 375°F [190°C/Gas Mark 5].

Bake the tart shells for 12 to 15 minutes or until golden brown. Let the tart shells cool completely in the pans on a rack before unmoulding them.

Chocolate Tart Dough

8 tablespoons [100g/4oz] unsalted butter, cut
  into 8 pieces
1 cup minus 2 tablespoons [90g/3 1/2oz]
  unbleached all-purpose [plain] flour
2 tablespoons plus 2 teaspoons unsweetened
  Dutch-processed cocoa powder

1/2 cup plus 2 tablespoons [65g/2 1/2oz]
  confectioners' sugar [icing sugar]
1 large egg yolk

Let the butter sit at room temperature for 10 to 15 minutes. It should be malleable but still cool.

Sift together the flour and cocoa powder.

Place the confectioners' sugar in the bowl of a food mixer or a medium mixing bowl. Add the butter and toss to coat. Using the paddle attachment, or a hand-held mixer, cream the sugar and butter at medium speed until the sugar is no longer visible. Scrape down the sides of the bowl. Add the egg yolk and beat until well blended. Scrape down the sides of the bowl again. Add half of the flour mixture and beat until the dough becomes crumbly. Stop the machine, add the remaining flour mixture, and beat until the dough forms a sticky mass. Shape the dough into a disc and wrap well in plastic. Refrigerate until firm, approximately 2 hours.

Roll out the dough, line the tart pans and bake as for Standard Tart Dough (above). To dust the work surface and rolling pin when working with chocolate dough, sift together 2 parts flour and 1 part cocoa powder. As the tarts are a deep shade of cocoa, colour won't help much to determine when they have finished baking. Engage your senses of smell and touch. A rich chocolate aroma and a dry interior mean the tart shells are done. If the tarts are close to being finished but you're not sure, pull them from the oven. It's fine to put them back in the oven if they do need additional time.

Lemon Meringue Tart, Manhattan Style

vegetable oil for the rings
6 Lemon Tarts made with Standard Tart Dough
  (see above)
6 large egg whites, at room temperature

1 teaspoon cream of tartar
1 cup [225g/8oz] granulated sugar
6 entremet rings, 3 inches [7.5cm] in diameter
  and 1¹/₂ inches [4cm] high

Lightly oil the inside of each entremet ring. Centre a ring on top of each tart and set aside.

Place the egg whites in the bowl of a food mixer or a large mixing bowl. Using the whisk attachment or a hand-held mixer, beat on low speed for 2 minutes. Add the cream of tartar, increase the speed to medium, and beat until soft peaks have formed. Gradually add the sugar in a steady stream and continue beating until stiff, glossy peaks have formed.

Spoon the meringue into the entremet rings, spreading it evenly over the tops of the tarts. Then dip the spoon into the meringue and quickly pull it up to create a small flourish on top of each tart.

Place the tarts in the freezer for at least 20 minutes or up to 4 hours.

To remove the entremet rings, gently shimmy them back and forth while sliding them off the meringue. Let the tarts sit at room temperature for 10 minutes before serving.

Cakes and Bakes

Dean Fearing

Date and Nut Chews

(Dean Fearing's Southwest Cuisine)

Dates and nuts are a familiar American combination: cream cheese sandwiches on date and nut bread enlivened many a lunchbox for me and my grade-school contemporaries. These chews – not totally dissimilar to flapjacks but a lot less chewy – are a homestyle American treat devised by Dean Fearing's pastry chef, Robert W. Zielinski. Fearing is one of the most stimulating chefs working in America. His reinterpretation of Tex-Mex and Southwestern American flavours for the well-heeled patrons of The Mansion at Turtle Creek Hotel in Dallas is showstopping. I've eaten three meals cooked by Dean and they rank among my most memorable. I admire the way he can go off into extraordinarily demanding flights of fancy and then come back down to earth with something like this which is both sophisticated and irresistibly childish. If you can't find corn syrup, use golden syrup instead.

Makes 36

¾ cup [75g/3oz] all-purpose [*plain*] flour
¼ teaspoon salt
2 large eggs
½ cup [100g/4oz] sugar
½ cup [120ml/4fl oz] corn syrup

½ teaspoon pure almond extract
1 cup [175g/6oz] finely chopped dates
1 cup [100g/4oz] chopped pecans
⅓ cup [35g/1¼oz] sifted confectioners' sugar [*icing sugar*]

Preheat oven to 375°F [*190°C/Gas Mark 5*].

Grease bottom of two 8 inch [*20cm*] square baking pans.

Sift flour with salt and set aside. In a mixing bowl, beat eggs with sugar, corn syrup and almond extract until light and fluffy. Stir in flour, dates and pecans and mix until well blended.

Pour batter into prepared pans and bake in preheated oven for 20 minutes or until done. Immediately cut into 1½ inch [*4cm*] squares. When squares have cooled slightly, roll into balls or fingers and coat with confectioners' sugar. Let cool before serving.

Jane Grigson

Italian Carrot and Almond Cake

(Jane Grigson's Vegetable Book)

Jane Grigson didn't horse around. Her recipes are short and sharp, laced with flashes of wit. Amongst her many admirable achievements was her determination that even, or perhaps especially, the most mundane ingredient should be treated with respect and intelligence. Has any carrot ever given its life more gloriously than as an ingredient in this cake? You will note that a mere tablespoon of flour is called for – just enough to hold the grated nuts, carrots and beaten eggs together – which makes it very light indeed.

Grating almonds calls for a little knowledge. Bathe the nuts in boiling water for a minute, then drain and leave to cool. The skin will peel off easily. If you have very little else to do you could grate them one by one on a coarse grater. Otherwise use a food processor but be sure not to turn them into powder. Jane Grigson suggests using a nut mill, which I assume is something like one of those little rotary graters you use for Parmesan. Or maybe it isn't. At any rate, I don't have one. By all means beat the egg whites stiffly, but do not beat them into a state of *rigor mortis* otherwise they will not blend smoothly. I would recommend beating them until they form a stiff peak that is still soft enough to waggle gently when shaken.

This cake is best attacked when just cool enough to eat. Serve it with soured cream or crème fraîche on top.

---

4 egg yolks
225g/8oz sugar
grated rind of a lemon
225g/8oz finely grated carrots
225g/8oz grated almonds

1 heaped tablespoon self-raising flour
4 egg whites, stiffly whipped
pine kernels (optional)
icing sugar

Beat the yolks, sugar and rind thoroughly together. This will take five minutes by hand, about half that with an electric beater. Mix in the carrots, almonds and flour. Fold in the whites gently with a metal spoon. Line a 5cm/2 inch pan, about 20cm/8 inches in diameter, with vegetable silicone parchment. Put in the cake mixture. If you have some pine kernels, sprinkle a heaped tablespoon over the top of the mixture before you put it into the oven. Pine kernels are always an improvement – nearly always, anyway – but the cake is really good without them. Bake at 180°C/350°F/Gas Mark 4 for about 45 minutes. Sprinkle with icing sugar before serving.

Katie Stewart

Plum Bread

(The Times Cookery Book)

One of our very best cookery writers, Katie Stewart was born in Scotland and studied domestic science there in Aberdeen. She appeals powerfully to my fantasy that all Scots women are magnificent bakers. Her recipes are classic, terribly British and frightfully well mannered. There is nothing she writes about that I do not want to cook or at the very least eat. If you like the idea of baking your own Christmas presents this plum bread can be made in huge batches and distributed to all the ageing aunties on your list who may be feeling overtaken by culinary fashions. Sliced thickly and buttered enthusiastically, it makes a terrific snack with a cup of very strong tea. It is also delicious served with a wedge of strong cheese such as Stilton.

Makes 2 large loaves

175g/6oz sultanas

100g/4oz glacé cherries

350g/12oz currants

175g/6oz seedless raisins

675g/1½lb self-raising flour

2 level teaspoons salt

1 level teaspoon mixed spice

225g/8oz butter

100g/4oz chopped mixed peel

350g/12oz caster sugar

600ml/1 pint warm milk

50g/2oz fresh yeast

Old-fashioned plum bread is fruity and rich. This bread keeps well and is better kept several days before serving.

Grease two large 23 x 13 x 5cm/9 x 5 x 2 inch loaf tins and line the base of each with a strip of greased paper. Wash and thoroughly pat dry the sultanas, cherries, currants and raisins. Cut the glacé cherries in half. Sift the flour, salt and mixed spice into a large mixing basin. Rub in the butter, add the prepared fruit, mixed peel and all but one teaspoon of sugar.

Dissolve the teaspoon of sugar in the warm milk and crumble the fresh yeast over the surface. Stir to mix. Make a well in the centre of the dried ingredients, add the yeast liquid all at once and gradually stir the mixture together to make a fairly stiff dough. Divide the mixture equally between the two prepared tins and spread evenly. Place in the centre of a low oven 150°C/350°F/Gas Mark 2 and bake for 2 hours. Allow the baked loaves to cool in the tins.

Serve sliced and buttered.

Note

This bread is not put to rise; the yeast is added to improve the keeping quality.

Ann and Franco Taruschio

Walnut Bread

(Leaves From The Walnut Tree)

A high degree of self-reliance – as much as possible made in the kitchen, as little as possible bought in – is often the mark of a great restaurant and, in the case of The Walnut Tree Inn in South Wales, is also part of the legacy from the days when it was the only restaurant of quality for many miles around. We home cooks are inclined to be a little lazy – especially when it comes to baking, surrounded as we are by so many tempting-looking breads in supermarkets and delicatessens. Still, even if you've got only the slightest inclination towards baking it's worth doing. Supposedly John Lennon said that baking a loaf of bread was one of the most creative things he'd ever done: I say 'supposedly' because a baker told me that story.

This recipe produces eight loaves, so unless you have a huge freezer or a very big family, just halve the quantities. It specifies Farina O flour, which you can find in Italian delicatessens. The bread is first rate with cheese or toasted for breakfast.

Makes 8 loaves

3kg/7lb Farina O flour
40g/1¹/₂oz sugar
50g/2oz salt
250g/9oz melted butter
1 glass extra virgin olive oil

200g/7oz yeast
650ml/22fl oz milk
carbonated mineral water
400g/14oz walnuts, roughly chopped
egg wash

Mix the flour, sugar, salt, melted butter and olive oil together. Dissolve the yeast in the milk. Add the milk and yeast to the flour mixture. Add the carbonated water.

Knead the mixture until a smooth dough is obtained. Leave the dough to rise for 1¹/₂ hours. Knead the dough briefly and cut into 8 pieces. Pass each piece of dough through a pasta machine until an oblong is obtained, about 1.25cm/¹/₂ inch thick.

Spread each oblong with roughly broken walnuts and roll up. Place the rolls in Hovis tins and leave to rise for 1 hour. Brush the dough with egg wash and bake for 30 minutes in an oven set at 190°C/375°F/Gas Mark 5. Place on the middle shelf.

This bread can be made with different fillings, such as chopped olives, olive paste, dried tomato paste, garlic and rosemary. It may seem a lot of bread to make but it freezes well.

Marvel Cream Cheese-Chocolate Brownies

(Dean Fearing's Southwest Cuisine)

Dean Fearing wears cowboy boots, says 'Howdy' and 'Y'all', looks like a Country and Western star and cooks as well as any much-starred Michelin chef. Even his fanciest food remains connected to the best American vernacular tastes. Every American family has its own 'special' recipe for brownies and this one comes from 'Dean's neighbour Gloria Shaw [who] won many contests at the state fair with this recipe, which brings a new meaning to brownies for the Nineties'. The cream cheese adds to the richness of the mix – and brownies are nothing if not almost too rich and gooey – but also lends a pleasantly sour note which keeps all that chocolate and sugar from being too cloying.

Makes 24

4 ounces [100g] unsweetened chocolate
1 cup [225g/8oz] unsalted butter
1/2 cup [100g/4oz] unsalted margarine
2 1/4 cups [275g/10oz] flour
1 teaspoon baking soda [*bicarbonate of soda*]
1/2 teaspoon salt
3 large eggs

1 teaspoon pure vanilla extract
2 cups [450g/1lb] sugar
1 cup [100g/4oz] chopped walnuts
1 cup [225g/8oz] cream cheese, softened
2 cups [225g/8oz] confectioners' sugar [*icing sugar*]

Preheat oven to 325°F [*160°C/Gas Mark 3*].

Grease and flour a 14 x 12 inch [*35 x 30cm*] sheet cake pan [*baking tin*].

Melt chocolate, 1/2 cup [*100g/4oz*] butter, and margarine in top half of a double boiler over boiling water, stirring to blend. When melted, remove from heat and allow to cool.

Sift together flour, baking soda and salt and set aside. In a mixing bowl, beat 2 eggs and vanilla until frothy. Add sugar and continue beating until thick and lemon-coloured. Gradually beat in flour mixture until well combined. Stir in chocolate mixture, scraping down sides of bowl as necessary. When well blended, pour into prepared pan. Smooth top and sprinkle with 1/2 cup [*50g/2oz*] walnuts. Set aside.

Beat cream cheese and remaining butter until light and fluffy. Add remaining egg and beat to combine. Add confectioners' sugar and beat until well blended.

Spread cream cheese mixture over top of brownies, leaving 1/2 inch [*1cm*] border all around, using a rubber spatula to smooth the surface. Sprinkle with remaining walnuts.

Place in preheated oven and bake for 30 to 40 minutes or until set.

Remove from oven and cool on a wire rack for 2 hours before cutting into squares.

Martha Stewart

Chocolate Devil's Food Cake

(The Martha Stewart Cookbook)

So called because it is as dark as can be, Devil's Food Cake stands alongside the River Café's Chocolate Nemesis (see page 192) as the absolute Grail for chocoholics. The recipe requires a little bit of translation for non-American cooks. You won't be able to find unsweetened chocolate so use dark chocolate with 70 per cent cocoa solids or Belgian continental chocolate. Buttermilk is splendid for all sorts of baking and is now popping up in some of our more enlightened supermarkets. You can substitute glucose or golden syrup for the corn syrup, unless you know a shop that specializes in imported American ingredients. You may be amused by another Americanism as Martha Stewart tells you to bake 'until a cake tester comes out clean'. What she calls a cake tester we call an old metal skewer dug out from the bottom of the drawer. The Seven-Minute Frosting is miraculous: slightly crispy on the outside, soft and marshmallowy within. By the way, the seven minutes just refers to the amount of time you're beating it over the heat; the whole operation takes about half an hour.

Try this as a birthday cake.

3 ounces [*75g*] unsweetened chocolate
1 teaspoon baking soda [*bicarbonate of soda*]
$^1/_2$ cup [*120ml/4fl oz*] boiling water
$^1/_2$ pound [*225g*] unsalted butter, at room temperature
2 cups [*450g/1lb*] sugar
5 eggs
3 cups [*350g/12oz*] all-purpose [*plain*] flour, sifted

$^3/_4$ cup [*175ml/6fl oz*] buttermilk
1 teaspoon vanilla extract
For the Seven-Minute Frosting:
$1^1/_2$ cups [*350g/12oz*] sugar
2 egg whites
$^1/_2$ cup [*120ml/4fl oz*] water
$^1/_8$ teaspoon salt
1 tablespoon light corn syrup
1 teaspoon vanilla extract

Preheat the oven to 350°F [*180°C/Gas Mark 4*]. Butter three 9 inch [*23cm*] round cake pans.

Melt the chocolate in a double boiler over simmering water. In a bowl, stir the baking soda into the $^1/_2$ cup [*120ml/4fl oz*] boiling water; stir this liquid into the chocolate. Set aside to cool slightly.

Using an electric mixer, cream the butter and sugar until the mixture is light and pale yellow in colour. Add the eggs, one at a time, and continue to mix until thoroughly incorporated. Alternately add the flour and buttermilk in small amounts, and blend well.

Add the melted chocolate and the vanilla to the batter and stir well. Pour the batter into the prepared pans and bake for 30 minutes or until a cake tester comes out clean when inserted into the centre of each cake. Remove the cakes from the oven and allow

them to cool briefly in the pans before inverting on to racks to cool thoroughly.

To make the frosting, in the top of a double boiler, combine the sugar, egg whites, water, salt, corn syrup and vanilla. Place over but not touching rapidly boiling water and beat with a whisk or electric mixer for exactly 7 minutes. Remove from the heat and continue beating until the frosting is cool, thick, and fluffy, about 20 to 25 minutes. Use immediately, as the frosting will harden as it cools.

Wolfgang Puck

Chocolate Chip Cookies

(The Wolfgang Puck Cookbook)

When I was growing up in New England, diligent mothers like my own seemed to bake cookies or brownies every afternoon for their children returning from school. Amongst all the arcane gooey, high-calorie treats with names like 123s (as easy to eat as 1 2 3) or smores (so good you had to have some more), the universal favourite was the chocolate chip cookie. In those days they were called Toll House Cookies, having supposedly first been baked along the old Boston to Providence toll road.

Wolfgang Puck's recipe is as good and easy as any chocolate chip cookie recipe ever devised. If you don't have chocolate chips, take a slab of plain chocolate and attack it with a heavy cook's knife. Nuts in chocolate chip cookies are a source of controversy and family strife. Pecans are luxurious, but perhaps a little too much for such a homely cookie. Almonds or walnuts are more populist. Peanuts are, I'm afraid, *infra dig*. Or you can skip the nuts altogether, which means that even those with a nut allergy can enjoy these cookies.

If you mix the dough in a food processor bear in mind the instruction to do it until *just* blended.

Chocolate chip cookies are best eaten slightly warm when they are still a bit soft and gooey. Serve with coffee or a glass of very cold milk. If you haven't baked your own cookies before, remember that they lack preservatives and will not keep as well as commercially baked ones. So eat them fresh and be damned.

Makes about 36

8 tablespoons [*100g/4oz*] unsalted butter
6 tablespoons [*75g/3oz*] sugar
6 tablespoons packed [*75g/3oz*] brown sugar
1 teaspoon vanilla
1/2 teaspoon salt
1 egg

2 2/3 cups [*275g/10oz*] plain flour, sifted
1/4 teaspoon baking soda [*bicarbonate of soda*] dissolved in 2 teaspoons hot water
1 cup [*100g/4oz*] chopped nuts
1 cup [*175g/6oz*] chocolate chips

Cream the butter in an electric mixer until light. With the mixer running slowly, add the sugar, brown sugar, vanilla, salt, egg, flour and dissolved baking soda. Mix until just blended. Stir in the chopped nuts and chocolate chips.

Preheat the oven to 350°F [*180°C/Gas Mark 4*]. If the dough is too soft, chill it until it stiffens a little. Then, shape balls of the dough 1 inch [*2.5cm*] in diameter and place them on a baking sheet, leaving 2 inches in between.

Bake the cookies for 15 to 17 minutes. They should be golden brown and only very slightly soft. Let the cookies cool on the sheet, then transfer them to a rack.

Store the cookies in an airtight container.

Gordon Ramsay

Apple Tuiles

(A Passion for Flavour)

I must admit that this is rather frivolous. But it is the sort of frivolity that is worth making, a) as a high-class snack for late-night television watching; b) to elevate ready-made ice cream or sorbet; c) to shut up your friends who go on a bit too much about what wonderful cooks they are. This recipe is both simple and highly professional. It's also the only reasonable thing you can do with Granny Smith apples, which I feel are pretty boring.

To begin, make a large batch of stock syrup, one of those chefly things that is actually worth keeping around. Put 550g/1¼lb granulated sugar and the grated zest of 1 lemon in a saucepan with 1 litre/1¾ pints water and heat slowly, stirring until the sugar has dissolved, then boil for 5 minutes. Let the syrup cool and then shove it in the fridge. Add a few cloves, cinnamon sticks or pieces of star anise for flavour, if you like. It is first rate spiked with a couple of dashes of Angostura bitters and poured over any fresh fruit.

Be sure to use nonstick silicone sheeting when you bake the apple slices: you can buy it from all professional chef shops and some better kitchen suppliers and you will find it useful for all sorts of things. You will have to watch the apple slices carefully as they bake because domestic ovens never have as cool a setting as professional ones. Consequently your apple slices will be slightly golden rather than virginally white: hardly worth a law suit. They are done when they look drier and are starting to shrivel. Don't get too worried about curling them, either over a rolling pin or in a baguette tin (which you are unlikely to have anyway). They look and taste just as good if they're flat.

2 Granny Smith apples
150ml/¼ pint stock syrup
juice of ½ lemon, strained

Neatly core the apples, making sure the coring is quite central. Pour the stock syrup into a bowl and mix with the lemon juice.

Using a mandoline or a very sharp knife, cut the apples into slices about 1mm/ ¹⁄₁₆ inch thick.

Drop these into the lemon syrup just to coat, then arrange in a single layer on a baking sheet lined with nonstick silicone baking sheeting.

Dry out in the oven on its lowest possible setting for about 2 hours, then remove the slices in relays and place them over a rolling pin to curl. If you remove them all at once they will crisp before you can curl them. Alternatively, if you have a French baguette tin, curl the slices inside the tubes. However, if you find curling difficult, bear in mind the slices also look attractive served flat.

Rose Levy Beranbaum

Cordon Rose Cream Cheesecake

(The Cake Bible)

You can buy ready-made products purporting to be 'American' or 'New York' cheesecake, none of which bears more than a passing resemblance to the real thing. New York is the cheesecake capital of the world and Rose Levy Beranbaum is the most articulate and fanatical advocate of New York cheesecake. 'I am passionate on the subject of cheesecake,' she declares and goes on to remark that, 'Cheesecake could really be classified more as a custard than as a cake. When this realization first hit me I decided to treat cheesecake as a custard and bake it in a water bath. To my delight, the result was perfectly creamy from stern to stern (without the usual dry outer edge).' Eureka!

This is a definitive recipe. If you have a food processor use Rose Levy Beranbaum's processor method, which is brilliantly simple. She suggests various biscuit bases but I agree with her conclusion that this cake can stand on its own. Amongst her many recommended variations I have selected Banana Cheesecake, which I think makes a nicely spoiling birthday cake.

Serves 8–12

two 8oz [225g] packets of cream cheese*
1 cup [225g/8oz] caster sugar
1 tablespoon cornflour (optional)†
3 large eggs

3 tablespoons freshly squeezed lemon juice
1½ teaspoons pure vanilla extract
¼ teaspoon salt
3 cups [750ml/1¼ pints] soured cream

*Don't be tempted to use the more expensive 'natural' cream cheese. Philadelphia brand, available even in Japan, offers the best and most consistent flavour for this cake.

†If cornflour is omitted, a small amount of liquid will seep out after unmoulding; this can be absorbed with a paper towel. I prefer not using the cornflour as the cake is a shade more creamy. Also, it makes it suitable to serve as a Passover dessert.

Preheat the oven to 350°F [*180°C/Gas Mark 4*].

Grease an 8 by 2¹/₂ inch [*20 x 6cm*] or higher springform tin and line the bottom with greased parchment or greaseproof paper. Wrap the outside of the tin with a double layer of heavy-duty foil to prevent seepage.

In a large mixing bowl beat the cream cheese and sugar until very smooth (about 3 minutes), preferably with a whisk beater. Beat in the cornflour if desired. Add the eggs, 1 at a time, beating after each addition until smooth and scraping down the sides. Add the lemon juice, vanilla and salt and beat until incorporated. Beat in the soured cream just until blended.

Pour the batter into the prepared tin. Set the tin in a larger tin and surround it with 1 inch [*2.5cm*] of very hot water. Bake for 45 minutes. Turn off the oven without opening the door and let the cake cool for 1 hour. Remove to a rack and cool to room temperature (about 1 hour). Cover with plastic wrap [*clingfilm*] and refrigerate overnight.

To unmould: have ready a serving plate and a flat plate at least 8 inches [*20cm*] in diameter, covered with plastic wrap. Place tin on heated burner and move it around for 15 seconds. Wipe sides of tin with a hot, damp towel.

Run a thin metal spatula around the sides of the cake and release the sides of the springform tin. Place the plastic-wrapped plate on top and invert. Remove the bottom of the tin and the parchment. Reinvert on to the serving plate and use a small metal spatula to smooth the sides. Refrigerate until shortly before serving.

Notes
An 8 by 3 inch [*20 x 7.5cm*] solid cake tin can be used instead of a springform. To unmould the cake, run a thin spatula around the sides, place the tin on heated burner for 10 to 20 seconds, moving the tin back and forth, and then invert. If the cake does not release, return to the hot burner for a few more seconds.

For a richer, denser cheesecake that completely holds its moisture without cornflour, replace the 3 whole eggs with 6 egg yolks.

Processor method
A food processor also works well to mix this batter. Process the cream cheese and sugar for 30 seconds or until smooth. Add the cornflour if desired and pulse to blend. Add the eggs, 1 at a time, with the motor running. Add the lemon juice, vanilla, salt and soured cream and pulse to combine.

Pointers for success
Wrapping the tin with foil keeps it watertight. Grease the sides of the tin so the surface will not crack when the cake starts to shrink on cooling. Chill thoroughly before unmoulding.

The water bath tin must not be higher than the springform tin or it will slow down baking.

Bottoms for cheesecake

Au naturel: This cheesecake is firm enough to be unmoulded and served without a base if desired.

Biscuit à la cuillère: Homemade or packaged ladyfingers [*sponge fingers*] can be used to line the bottom and sides of the cake tin. Use a 9 by 3 inch [*23 x 7.5cm*] tin and butter to grease the sides of the tin; this holds the ladyfingers in position. After baking 25 minutes, cover the top of the cheesecake loosely with foil to prevent over-browning. Before unmoulding, wipe the outside of the tin with a hot, wet towel.

Cookie crumb crust: Ginger, graham and lemon-nut cookies go well with fruit-flavoured fillings or toppings. As crumb crusts become soggy if placed in the tin before baking, I prefer to pat the crumbs on to the cake after baking and unmoulding. You will need about ³/₄ cup [*75g/3oz*] if you wish to do the bottom as well as the sides.

Banana Cheesecake

Anyone who has ever eaten bananas and soured cream and loved it will know before even tasting this cake just how mellow and delicious it's going to be. The bananas seem to have some preserving quality as well because this cake stays fresh-tasting for at least 12 days! Bananas and soured cream have about the same moisture content so all you do is replace one-third of the soured cream with mashed banana.

To make Banana Cheesecake: Replace 1 cup [*250ml/8fl oz*] soured cream with 1 cup [*225g/8oz*] mashed banana. (You will need 2 very ripe bananas.) To keep the banana from discolouring, stir the 3 tablespoons of lemon juice into the mashed banana. Blend into the batter after the soured cream is incorporated.

Acknowledgements

From Loyd Grossman

This book would not have been possible without the amazing diligence and hard work of Roz Denny, who did the recipe research.

From the publishers

The publishers wish to thank the copyright-holders of the following recipes for permission to reprint them in this volume.

Baba Ghannooge, Chicken Wings Marinated in Garlic and Yoghurt and Cucumber Salad: from *Lebanese Cuisine* by Anissa Helou, published by Grub Street, London; copyright © Anissa Helou. • Hummus bi Tahini, Falafel or Ta'Amia and Pissaladière: from *Mediterranean Cookery;* copyright © Claudia Roden, 1987; by permission of the BBC. • Silver Dollar Corn Cakes and Peppered Tuna: from *Fresh Start* by Julee Rosso; copyright © Julee Rosso, 1996; by permission of Crown Publishers, Inc. • Fried Halloumi Cheese with Lime and Caper Vinaigrette: from *Delia Smith's Summer Collection* by Delia Smith; copyright © Delia Smith, 1993; by permission of the BBC. • Pasta e Fagioli and Walnut Bread: from *Leaves from the Walnut Tree* by Ann and Franco Taruschio; copyright © Ann and Franco Taruschio, 1993; by permission of Pavilion Books. • Cream of Spinach Soup: from *The Cuisine of Hungary* by George Lang (Penguin Books, 1985); copyright © George Lang, 1971; by permission of Penguin Books Ltd. • Curried Butternut Squash Soup: from *The Silver Palate Cookbook*; copyright © Julee Rosso & Sheila Lukins, 1982; by permission of Workman Publishing Company, Inc. • Huevos Rústicos and Codornices Asadas en Mole de Cacahuale: from *Rick Bayless's Mexican Kitchen* by Rick Bayless, published by Absolute Press, Bath, England; copyright © Richard Lane Bayless, 1996; with the permission of Scribner, a Division of Simon & Schuster. • Classic Cheese Soufflé: from *The Cook's Companion,* published by Websters International Publishers; copyright © Josceline Dimbleby, 1991. • A Traditional Recipe for Blini and Gurevskie Blini: from *The Food and Cooking of Russia* by Lesley Chamberlain, published by Penguin Books; copyright © Lesley Chamberlain, 1982; by permission of Penguin Books Ltd. • Pasticcio Macaronia: from *The Best Book of Greek Cookery* by Chrissas Paradissis; copyright © Efstathiadis Group SA. • Tagliolini Gratinati al Prosciutto, Salsa Besciamella and Risotto Parmigiano: from *The Harry's Bar Cookbook* by Arrigo Cipriani; copyright © by Arrigo Cipriani Inc, 1991; produced by The Miller Press; by permission of Bantam Books, a division of Bantam Doubleday Dell Publishing Group, Inc. • Egg Noodles with Tofu and Yam Pla Muek: from *Healthy Thai Cooking* by Sri Owen, published by Frances Lincoln Ltd; copyright © Sri Owen, 1997; by permission of Frances Lincoln Ltd, 4 Torriano Mews, Torriano Avenue, London, NW5 2RZ. • Pasta con la Mollica, Pizza Rustica and Insalata Arriganata: from *Southern Italian Cooking* by Valentina Harris; copyright © Valentina Harris, 1993; by permission of Pavilion Books. • Polenta, Polenta alla Griglia and Chocolate Nemesis: from *The River Café Cook Book* by Ruth Rogers and Rose Gray, published by Ebury Press; copyright © Ruth Rogers and Rose Gray, 1995. • Addas Polow: from *Legendary Cuisine of Persia* by Margaret Shaida, published by Lieuse Publications; copyright © Margaret Shaida, 1992. • Kedgeree: from *Fine English Cookery* by Michael Smith, published by BBC Books; copyright © Michael Smith, 1973. • Pizza with Shrimp and Sun-dried

Tomatoes, Pizza Dough and Chocolate Chip Cookies: from *The Wolfgang Puck Cookbook* by Wolfgang Puck; copyright © Wolfgang Puck, 1986; by permission of Random House, Inc. • La (Vraie) Salade Niçoise: from *Cuisine Niçoise: Recipes from a Mediterranean Kitchen* by Jacques Médecin, translated by Peter Graham, published by Penguin Books; copyright © Juillard, 1972; this translation copyright © Penguin Books Ltd, 1983. • Oriental Salad and Bread and Butter Pudding: from *Roast Chicken and Other Stories* by Simon Hopkinson with Lindsey Bareham, published by Random House; copyright © Simon Hopkinson, 1994. • Oven-cured Tomatoes, Cornmeal Pan-fried Green Tomatoes and Tomato Sandwiches: from *Lee Bailey's Tomatoes* by Lee Bailey; copyright © Lee Bailey, 1992; by permission of Clarkson N. Potter, Inc., a division of Crown Publishers, Inc., and William Morris Agency, Inc. on behalf of the author. • Caesar Salad: from *From Julia Child's Kitchen* by Julia Child; copyright © Julia Child, 1975; by permission of Alfred A. Knopf, Inc. • Mayonnaise and Summer Pudding: from *Summer Cooking* by Elizabeth David, published by Penguin Books; copyright © the Estate of Elizabeth David, 1955, 1965, 1988; by kind permission of Jill Norman. • Gratin de Navets and Gratin Dauphinois: from *Simple French Food* by Richard Olney; published by Penguin Books; copyright © Richard Olney, 1974. • Spanakopita: from *Greek Cooking* by Robin Howe; copyright © Robin Howe; by permission of André Deutsch Ltd. • Ratatouille: from *Mediterranean Food* by Elizabeth David, published by Penguin Books; copyright © the Estate of Elizabeth David, 1950, 1955, 1958, 1965, 1988 and 1991; by kind permission of Jill Norman. • Tarte aux Oignons d'Alsace and Potato Latkes: from *The Book of Jewish Food* by Claudia Roden, published by Viking; copyright © Claudia Roden, 1997. • Parmigiana di Melanzane and Spumone di Zabaglione: from *Secrets from an Italian Kitchen* by Anna del Conte, published by Transworld Publishers; copyright © Anna del Conte, 1989. • Roast Potatoes and Banana Tarts: from *Real Cooking* by Nigel Slater, published by Michael Joseph; copyright © Nigel Slater, 1997; by permission of Penguin Books Ltd. • Spinach with Butter, Fish Soup with Croûtons and Salmon Marinated in Dill: from *Rick Stein's Taste of the Sea* by Rick Stein; copyright © Richard Stein, 1995; by permission of BBC Books. • Stir-fried Asparagus, Scallion 'Exploded' Lamb and Chicken Fu Yung Sauce for Vegetables: from *The Key to Chinese Cooking* by Irene Kuo; copyright © Irene Kuo, 1977; by permission of Alfred A. Knopf, Inc. • Grand Prize Chilli: from Great Chefs Televison's companion cookbook to the 'Great Chefs of the West' series entitled *Southwest Tastes* (www.greatchefs.com); recipe copyright © Ray Calhoun. • Yankee Pot Roast and Maine Crabmeat Turnovers: from *Jasper White's Cooking from New England*; copyright © Jasper White, 1989; by permission of Jasper White. • Kalio: from *Red Heat* by Maureen Suan-Neo; copyright © Maureen Suan-Neo. • Leg of Lamb Andalusian Style and Estouffade of Goat: from *The Real Meat Cookbook* by Frances Bissell, published by Chatto & Windus; copyright © Frances Bissell, 1992. • Pla Moo: from *Vatch's Thai Cookbook* by Vatcharin Bhumichitr; copyright © Vatcharin Bhumichitr, 1994; by permission of Pavilion Books. • The Epicure's Kidneys: from *Margaret Costa's Four Seasons Cookery Book* by Margaret Costa, published by Grub Street, London; copyright © Margaret Costa, 1970. • Involtini con Funghi: from *A Passion for Mushrooms* by Antonio Carluccio, published by Pavilion Books; copyright © Antonio Carluccio, 1987; by permission of the author c/o Rogers, Coleridge & White Ltd, 20 Powis Mews, London, W11 1JN. • Poulet Sauté: from *Mastering the Art of French Cooking* by Julia Child, Simone Beck and Louisette Bertholle; copyright © Alfred A. Knopf, Inc., 1961; by permission of the publisher. • Stir-fried Chicken with Ginger, Cardamom and Cashew Nuts: extracted from *Suppers* by Claire Macdonald, published by Doubleday, a division of Transworld Publishers Ltd; copyright © Lady Macdonald of Macdonald, 1994; all rights reserved. • Chicken Kdra with Almonds and Chickpeas: from *Couscous and Other Good Food from Morocco* by Paula Wolfert, published by Grub Street, London; copyright © Paula Wolfert, 1973. • Roast Chicken with Lemons and Grilled Fish, Romagna Style: from *The Essentials of Classic Italian Cooking* by Marcella Hazan, published by Macmillan General Books. • Shichimi-spiced Duck and Escarole Salad with Ginger Vinaigrette and Quince and Polenta Crumble: from *The Fusion* by Martin Webb and Richard Whittington, published by Ebury; copyright © Martin Webb and Richard Whittington. • Canard aux Pêches: from *Memories of Gascony* by Pierre Koffman; copyright © Pierre Koffman; by permission of the author. • Provençal Rabbit Stew with Olives and Capers: from *The Dean & Deluca Cookbook* by David Rosengarten with Joel Dean and Giorgio DeLuca; copyright © Dean and Deluca, Inc.,

1996; by permission of Random House, Inc. •
Salmon Fishcake with Sorrel Sauce: from *The Ivy*
by A. A. Gill, Christopher Corbin and Jeremy
King; first published in 1997 by Hodder and
Stoughton, a division of Hodder Headline plc;
copyright © A. A. Gill, Christopher Corbin and
Jeremy King, 1997; by permission of Hodder and
Stoughton Limited. • Salmon Wrapped in
Courgette Ribbons with Tomato Vinaigrette:
from *Gourmet Ireland Two* by Paul and Jeanne
Rankin, published by BBC Books; copyright ©
Paul and Jeanne Rankin. • Cod with a Parsley
Crust: from *Rhodes Around Britain* by Gary
Rhodes, published by BBC Books; copyright ©
Gary Rhodes, 1994. • Salt Cod with Tomatoes
and Pesto: from *Real Good Food* by Nigel Slater;
copyright © Nigel Slater, 1993, 1994 and 1995; by
permission of Fourth Estate Ltd. • Vatroushka
with Smoked Salmon: from *The Cooking of Russia*,
a Sainsbury Cookbook, by Karen Craig and Seva
Novgorodsev, published by Martin Books, a
division of Simon & Schuster London. • Smoked
Haddock Pie: from *First Slice Your Cookbook* by
Arabella Boxer; copyright © Arabella Boxer, 1964;
by permission of the author c/o Rogers,
Coleridge & White Ltd, 20 Powis Mews, London,
W11 1JN. • Queue de Lotte Rôtie à la Moutarde
et Estragon and Clafoutis aux Cerises: from
Cooking for Friends by Raymond Blanc, published
by Headline Book Publishing Ltd; copyright ©
Raymond Blanc, 1991. • Roasted Brill with a
Brandade of Cod and Apple Tuiles: from *A Passion
for Flavour* by Gordon Ramsay, published by
Conran Octopus; copyright © Gordon Ramsay. •
Rendez-vous de Fruits-de-Mer à la Crème de
Basilic: from *Cuisine à la Carte* by Anton
Mosimann; copyright © Anton Mosimann; by
kind permission of Anton Mosimann. • Pecan Pie
and Pumpkin Pie: from *American Sampler*, a
Sainsbury Cookbook (reprinted as *The Cooking
of the USA*, 1990), published by Martin Books, a
division of Simon & Schuster London; copyright
© Patricia Lousada, 1985; by permission of the
publishers. • Swedish Cream: from *The Ark
Restaurant Cookbook* by Jimella Lucas and Nanci
Main; by kind permission of the authors. • Light
Christmas Pudding: from *Delicious Home Cooking*
by Caroline Conran, published by Conran
Octopus; copyright © Caroline Conran, 1992; by
permission of Conran Octopus. • Sticky Toffee
Pudding: from *The Cook's Companion* by Stephanie
Alexander, published by Penguin Books Australia;
copyright © Stephanie Alexander. • Gelato di
Cappuccino and Gelato di Panna: from *Marcella's
Kitchen* by Marcella Hazan, published by
Macmillan General Books. • Jerry's Chocolate
Ice Cream: from *Ben & Jerry's Homemade Ice
Cream and Desserts Book* by Ben Cohen and Jerry
Greenfield; copyright © Ben Cohen and Jerry
Greenfield, 1987; by permission of Workman
Publishing Company, Inc. • Apple Brown Betty
and Philadelphia Ice Cream: from *Soul Food* by
Sheila Ferguson, published by Weidenfeld &
Nicolson; copyright © Sheila Ferguson. • Brown
Bread Ice Cream with Rum: from *Michael Smith's
New English Cookery* by Michael Smith, published
by BBC Books; copyright © Michael Smith, 1985.
• Strawberries Romanov, Peaches with Raspberry
Purée and Drunken Watermelon: from *The Theory
and Practice of Good Cooking* by James Beard;
copyright © James Beard, 1977; by permission of
The Estate of the Late James Beard and A. M.
Heath & Co. Ltd. • Pistachio Crème Brûlée:
from *Desserts – A Lifelong Passion* by Michel Roux,
published by Conran Octopus; copyright ©
Michel Roux. • Bakewell Pudding: from
Traditional Dishes of Britain by Philip Harben,
published by The Bodley Head; copyright ©
Philip Harben. • Lemon Tart Four Ways: from
The Book of Tarts by Maury Rubin; copyright ©
Maury Rubin, 1995; by permission of William
Morrow & Company, Inc. • Date and Nut
Chews and Marvel Cream Cheese-Chocolate
Brownies: from *Dean Fearing's Southwest Cuisine*
by Dean Fearing; copyright © by Rosewood
Property Company, 1990; by permission of
Grove/Atlantic, Inc. • Italian Carrot and Almond
Cake: from *Jane Grigson's Vegetable Book* by Jane
Grigson, published by Michael Joseph; copyright
© Jane Grigson, 1978, 1979. • Plum Bread: from
The Times Cookery Book by Katie Stewart,
published by HarperCollins Publishers Ltd;
copyright © Katie Stewart.

Every effort has been made to contact copyright-holders of material in this book.
The publishers would be glad to be told of anyone who has not been consulted,
so that these omissions can be rectified in any future editions.

Index